A Punjabi Village in Pakistan

A PUNJABI

VILLAGE

IN PAKISTAN

BY ZEKIYE EGLAR

COLUMBIA   UNIVERSITY   PRESS

NEW YORK 1960

Clarke F. Ansley Award

This study, prepared
under the Graduate Faculties of Columbia University,
was selected by a committee of those Faculties
to receive one of the Clarke F. Ansley awards
given annually by Columbia University Press.

For Ruth Benedict

Foreword

One of the principal difficulties an anthropologist must face involves the question of how to establish distance—enough and not too much—between the field worker and the people whose life is to be studied and described. If we do not come to know the people as individuals, some of whom are loved and preferred above others, we can have little hope of understanding the culture which they embody. So we have come to depend upon the distance between two ways of life, which may be thousands of years apart, to give us the necessary objectivity. And the closer we come to our own culture, the more we must depend upon habits of observation established in studies of remote and primitive peoples to temper our identifications and preserve a modicum of noninvolvement.

The difficulty is compounded for the field worker who studies not a primitive people but a traditional community whose members belong to one of the great religions—Buddhism, Judaism, Islam, or one of the worldwide Christian groups. In this situation questions of belief, sincerity, compromise, and loyalty to his own faith, or to a sturdy and convinced rejection of the faith of his ancestors, all perplex the field worker, and he must decide whether to "bow down to wood and stone" or, in the interests of understanding and empathy, to violate some firmly held religious or antireligious position. The difficulty is further compounded in a culture in which the roles of men and women are very different—where there are mysteries that are reserved for one sex or where the sphere of activities of one sex is severely circumscribed.

This study of a Punjabi village is unique because it has been made by a woman anthropologist among a group of people who share the religious faith in which she was reared but who live far away—in Pakistan. Here the empathy provided by a common religious background and the entree given her, because she is a Muslim woman, into the closed aspects the lives of the women could be combined with the distance contributed by her different background in the Caucasus and Turkey and the role accorded her as a scholar with Western training. Because of this she could confidently pursue her task—moving freely from the position of an honored guest who was treated respectfully by the men to that of a trusted confidant who could be admitted to the women's quarters, and always attending to the children who shuttled back and forth between the two worlds. The relationships described in this study are even now being drastically changed by the land reforms that are under way.

A combination of international complications and the great hospitality of her host in the village of Mohla gave her a longer period of field work than our present system of grants and field funds would have underwritten. As we owe the fullness of *Argonauts of the Western Pacific* to the accident of Bronislaw Malinowski's internment during the First World War, so, too, we can be grateful for those accidents of history which, while they placed a burden on Dr. Eglar and her host, have given us a record of the traditional, now rapidly changing life of a village which would never have been obtained during the more usual brief field trip. In the pace and depth of the writing the reader and student are given a dimension seldom present, that of time.

MARGARET MEAD

American Museum of Natural History, New York
November 2, 1959

Preface

This is a study of village life in the Punjab. The people studied are Muslims, and the locus of the study is the village of Mohla, in Gujrat district, the neighboring villages which, together with Mohla, form a loosely organized cluster, and a few more distant villages which are linked to Mohla mainly through ties of marriage. Emphasis is placed on one of the institutions important in the traditional life of the village people—*vartan bhanji,* a complex mechanism for the exchange of gifts and services—which has served as a principal means of integration in this society.

The observations on which this study is based were made during a trip to West Pakistan, where I did field work for over five years —from the latter part of 1949 until March 1955. My choice of Pakistan as the country in which to do field work was determined by the fact of my being both a woman anthropologist and a Muslim.

In October 1958 there was a change of government in Pakistan. The new government has introduced revolutionary changes in the system of land tenure and ownership, the system of education, the legal system, economic policies, refugee rehabilitation, and administration. Among these the agrarian reforms will have the most significant effect upon the landowning class. The present study is concerned with the village life as it existed prior to these recent reforms.

The partition of united India and the establishment of Pakistan as a new state took place in August, 1947. In carrying on their struggle for an independent state, the Muslims of India had claimed a cultural heritage distinct from that of the Hindus, and they wanted a country in which Muslims would be given an opportunity to survive as a cultural entity. Whereas outsiders tended to see the Muslims of India in terms of the cultural heritage which they shared with the other peoples of India, Muslims, even though they shared many local customs, did not identify themselves with Hindus but wanted to assert their consciousness of belonging to the larger brotherhood of Islam. The establishment of the new Muslim state and the creation of the new Muslim nation, it was evident, would lead to immediate social and cultural change, and the study of this changing society had an immediate appeal to me as an anthropologist.

Pakistan appealed to me also because of my background and training. My childhood was spent in the southern Caucasus where, under the Russian Czarist regime, various ethnic groups felt their cultural identity very intensely. However, while the Georgians called themselves Georgians and the Armenians felt themselves to be Armenians, the Muslims of the southern Caucasus identified themselves with the world of Islam in general and with the Turks of the Ottoman Empire in particular. Although we spoke Russian and our family friends were Russian, our home was essentially a Muslim home. Our visits to my maternal grandfather made an indelible impression upon me as a Muslim: there, great respect for the elders, hospitality, abundant charity, and distance between the sexes were stressed as part of our religion, and there prayer, fasting, and religious holidays were an important part of our life.

My family escaped from Soviet Russia to Turkey, where we settled. This was the beginning of a period during which we became keenly aware of cultural differences because of the constant comparisons made by adults between the ways of our native country and Turkish ways of life, differences which we felt the more deeply because of our earlier identification with the Turks. Then, too, as a result of the reforms of Ataturk, with their Westernizing effects, Turkish society presented a picture of a people in various stages of rapid cultural change. The changes in our own lives and our experience with the ongoing change in Turkey both contributed to my interest in becoming a student of culture.

By going to Pakistan in 1949, I considered that field work would give me an opportunity to study both the traditional culture and the effect of changes as they took place. I decided to study village culture in Punjab, for the Punjab is regarded as the heart of West Pakistan and has the tradition of having been settled for a longer time than the other provinces of Pakistan. Whereas in some societies it is disadvantageous for a woman alone to do field work, I felt that in making a study of a Muslim society my being a woman would be an advantage for I would be accepted by both men and women.

My first stop in Pakistan was Lahore, at that time the provincial capital of the Punjab. There I was introduced, through Dr. Marian Smith, to Mr. Muhammad Sadullah, Director of the Government Archives; through his assistance it was possible for me to use the records in the Archives and the Library of the Secretariat. For background, I read the Government Gazetteers, various economic surveys, and a number of books on the administration, castes, and life of the Punjabi villages. In Lahore, I also met several families, attended a few marriages and other religious ceremonies, and made an initial acquaintance with the urban culture.

My main purpose, however, was to settle in a village. In this connection I had to face two problems: language and the choice of a village. The official languages of Pakistan are Urdu and English, and in Lahore all educated people speak English. (Since this field work was completed, Bengali has been accepted also as an official language.) But in the villages of the Punjab people speak Punjabi, and although, according to a Punjabi proverb, "language changes every fifteen miles," there is a basic Punjabi which people understand throughout this province. At first I was advised to study

Urdu, for Punjabi could be learned only by living among the people, not by formal instruction; besides, I was told, there would be in every village some man who spoke Urdu. Although I did study Urdu, it was clear to me that I needed to move to a village and to learn Punjabi.

While I was living in Lahore, I made several visits to villages in its immediate vicinity and also to Kasur, forty miles northeast of Lahore. These villages did not suit me because of their proximity to the city and also because, in most of them, the population had radically changed after the Partition, as Hindus and Sikhs left and refugees arrived from various provinces in India. Besides, Kasur was too near the disturbed border. I wanted to find a village at some distance from Lahore with a predominantly Muslim population which had not been seriously disturbed by the political upheavals which preceded the Partition of August, 1947.

For purposes of administration, Punjab had been divided into twenty-nine districts. After the Partition, twelve were annexed by India and seventeen remained within the boundaries of Pakistan. (Later, on October 14, 1955, these districts of the Punjab and the other provinces merged into one unit, West Pakistan; but at the time of my field work, the Punjab was a separate province.) Some of the districts, settled for a longer time than others, are considered to be typical of the whole province. The district of Gujrat is one of these, and it was there that I decided to go.

A family in Lahore introduced me to a businessman from Gujrat who owned land in a village at some distance from the city of Gujrat, where I was welcome to stay. Also, the Director of Public Relations in Lahore wrote to the Deputy Commissioner of Gujrat; the Deputy Commissioner, who was to leave soon for a tour of the villages in his district offered to take me along.

The problem of language would be more difficult in Gujrat, so I was advised to take along an interpreter to help me at least for a brief period. But to find someone who spoke both English and Punjabi and who would be interested in spending some time in a strange village seemed almost impossible. Finally, an official in the Public Relations office told me that one of his cousins, a young landowner and a college graduate, to whom he had spoken about my difficulties, was willing to help me. I was to meet him in Gujrat in February, 1950.

I left Lahore in the first week of February to visit the village in which the businessman in Gujrat owned land. This village was seven miles from the city, right on the highway, and could be reached by horse and buggy. I stayed there for one week before I decided that it was not suitable for field work. Aside from the fact that I had to make special arrangements to obtain my food from the city, the house I lived in was located outside the village in an orchard of mangoes and oranges, so, though my surroundings were beautiful, I was cut off from the villagers. In addition, the man who owned most of the land in the village lived in the city, the village was populated mainly by *kammis*, craftsmen, and the social structure of this village was not typical for the Punjab.

On February 20, I returned to the city of Gujrat, where I was joined by Chowdhri Fazl Ahmad, the young *zamindar*, landowner, who had volunteered to help me, and we left with the Deputy Commissioner on a tour of the villages in the district of Gujrat. I found a village which appealed to me in the *tahsil* of Phalia, a subdivision of the district, fifty miles from the city of Gujrat, and the Deputy Commissioner left me in the care of the all-powerful *zamindar* of that area. In that village I remained for three weeks, living in the women's quarters with the wife and children of the *zamindar*, while my interpreter stayed in the men's guest house. Living with the women, I was able to observe them at all times and to communicate with them by signs and a few words of Urdu. However, there were a number of drawbacks for a prolonged stay and study in this village. As all of the land belonged to branches of one family, there were no other *zamindars* in the village and the tenants did not feel at ease in speaking to me or to my interpreter. Furthermore, as the interpreter was an outsider, he could not move about freely—he had to avoid most of the women and could speak with only a few of them.

When I expressed dissatisfaction over my choice, my interpreter suggested that I visit the village where he owned land. In this way I came to Mohla, the village where I settled down to study rural life in the Punjab. This village and those immediately around it had not been seriously disturbed by the Partition. Three miles away from Mohla, in a village where there is a market, there had been Hindus and Sikhs who left and some refugees who came to settle, but this had not been the case in Mohla or the villages nearby. As this village was within easy reach of Gujrat, I was able to make several visits to the Office of the Deputy Commissioner, where I studied Urdu manuscripts on the history of Mohla, the landhold-ings and inheritance. By this means I could place Mohla in a his-torical context.

Among the several *zamindar* families in Mohla, the family of my interpreter owned most of the land, and one of his ancestors founded the village. For generations, therefore, this family has had the status of *chowdhri,* village chieftain. In the village I was ac-cepted unquestioningly by men and women alike. That I was in-vited to stay by the *chowdhri* and that his family lived in the village were great advantages. The *chowdhri* understood that I had come to study village life. He had accompanied me to the second village I visited and, having realized the difficulties one encounters on such an enterprise, wanted to help me. As for the village people, the men were amused and the women were puzzled about "what there was to learn about them, especially by an educated person who had come from such a distance." The fact that I was a Turk and a Muslim pleased people both in the cities and in the villages, for the Muslims of Pakistan have cherished a great love for the Turks and have shown much interest in Turkey.

For the first two months I lived in the *chowdhri's* guest house, often visiting the main house, where his womenfolk lived—his mother, his sisters, and the widow of his elder brother—with the children and the servants. I spent the summer away from Mohla. In September, when I returned, there was a big flood. Many of the mud houses were demolished, and water in the guest house rose to four feet. I moved to the main house which was built on higher ground. As the water kept rising, some of the village women and their children took refuge there also, while others left the village. The *chowdhri* intended to send his whole family and me away to safety, but when his mother refused to leave because this would dishearten the rest of the people, I felt I could not leave either. People felt that this action was proof that I was a "noble" person— *sherif*, as the old *chowdhrani*, the mother of the *chowdhri*, said. After the flood subsided, I lived for several weeks with the women; we became friendly and the children began spontaneously to call me *Apaji*, older sister, which gave me a place in the family circle. After that, I lived as it was convenient for my work—sometimes in the guest house and sometimes with the women.

The guest house of the *chowdhri* is the center of men's activities in the village. On the other hand, in the main house there is the daily routine of work and a constant flow of women visitors, who bring news of what goes on in the village, in the neighboring villages, among the men, among the women. Then there is always some extra activity going on—taking care of the produce that comes from the fields, spinning thread for the cotton blankets which are used for bedding or given away, preparing for visits by relatives from distant villages, and getting ready to attend ceremonial occasions among relatives.

At first the *chowdhri* translated for me as people talked, but after a few months I was able to participate fully in what was going on. An essential part of the people's life, especially that of the women, is to attend the various ceremonies among their relatives. My stay, therefore, was not confined to Mohla. Together with the women, I traveled and stayed for days in many villages within a radius of 150 miles. Or together with the *chowdhrani* and a group of *zamindar* and *kammi* women, I went to offer condolences in neighboring villages as was required by custom. As I grew more familiar with their ways and knew the standards required for marriage, I was asked to accompany women and give my opinion about the eligibility of young men and their families for a young daughter who was of marriageable age. As time passed, I was able to understand the undercurrents of events, and many subtleties of the culture became meaningful to me. I could understand the great emphasis placed on maintaining proper relations with all the people with whom one deals in life, and I could appraise the significance in their lives of the complex gift exchange which was to become the dominant subject of this study.

I traveled extensively in West Pakistan for my work as well as to become acquainted with the different parts of the country. I visited villages in the districts of Lahore, Gujrat, Gujranwala, Sialkot, Lyallpur, Multan, and Sargodha; I spent six months in Sind, where the Punjabis have settled in new villages and have established businesses; I also visited the provinces of Baluchistan, the North-West Frontier Province, the tribal area, the states of Dir and Swat, the northernmost state of Chitral, where I lived for one month; and I spent part of one summer in the valley of Kaghan, a western extension of Kashmir Valley. Thus, in the course of time, I came to see Mohla and its cluster of neighboring villages in the larger context of the area.

The plan for my field work in Pakistan was made with the help and advice of the late Professor Ruth Benedict; I owe my deepest gratitude to her as a teacher and a guide in my development as an anthropologist. I am thankful to Professor Margaret Mead, whose advice and steady encouragement during the years in which I lived and worked in Pakistan kept me at my work and helped me to see beyond it to a time when I would return to the United States and bring together this research. For his continuing interest and support, I wish to express my gratitude to Dr. Philip Mosely.

For the financial support which made this extended field work possible, I wish to thank the Social Science Research Council for the Area Research Training Fellowship which I held in 1949–1950 and which was renewed in 1950–1951; I wish also to thank the Wenner-Gren Foundation for Anthropological Research for a grant made to me for work in 1949–1950; and I wish to thank the Institute for Intercultural Studies for grants which enabled me to complete my field work. Preparation of this material for publication was made possible through a Research Fellowship for the spring session of 1958, which was granted by the Near and Middle East Institute of Columbia University.

The anthropologist traveling in a country as a stranger but as one who, through his work, hopes to understand that country well is singularly dependent upon all those who, with knowledge, advice, and above all good will, are able to set him on the right path and to smooth the difficulties along the way. Yet it is never possible to acknowledge in full one's indebtedness or even to mention all those whose help makes meaningful field work possible. This is especially the case for someone like myself, who has had the privilege to enjoy the hospitality of Pakistan for five years.

Nevertheless, I wish especially to express my gratitude to the following rulers and governors of states: H.H. the Nawab of Dir and H.H. the Heir Apparent of Dir, who was most kind to me; H.H. Saif-ur-Rahman, the late Mehtar of Chitral; H. H. Prince Ased-ur-Rahman, brother of the late Mehtar of Chitral and Governor of Torkho in the State of Chitral; H.H. Prince Hussam-ul-Mulk, Governor of Drosh, in the state of Chitral; H.H. Prince Meta-ul-Mulk, Governor of Khozere, in the state of Chitral; Mr. Shams-ul-Din, President of the Council, in the state of Chitral; and H.H. the Wali of Swat.

I wish also to thank especially Sardar Abdul Rab Nishtar, Governor of the Punjab; Mr. Akhtar Hussain, Financial Commissioner of the Punjab; Syed Fida Hussain, Commissioner of Lahore; Mr. Riaz Uddin Ahmed, Deputy Commissioner of Gujrat; Mr. Muhammad Sadullah, Director of Government Archives, Lahore; Syed Nur Ahmad, Director of Public Relations, Lahore; Malik M. Yusaf and

Chowdhri Sejjad Haider of the Office of Public Relations, Lahore; Mr. Muiz-ud-Din Ahmad, Chief Secretary of the North-West Frontier Province; Major Muhammad Yusuf, Political Agent of the states of Dir, Swat, and Chitral; Mr. Mir Ajem, Assistant Political Agent of the state of Chitral; Mr. Zafar-u-Zaman, Assistant Political Agent of the agency of Parachinar; and Mr. Abdul Kadir, Curator of the museum at Texila.

I wish also to express my gratitude to the following families and individuals for their warm hospitality: Dr. George J. Candreva, USIS officer in Lahore, and Mrs. Candreva; Syed Muhammad Hayat, the chief of Kaghan Valley, and his family in whose house I lived while in Kaghan; Head Constable Pir Muhammad Shah, stationed at Kaghan; Chowdhri Ghulam Dastegir and his brother, Haji Anyet Ali, of the village of Gudyala, district of Sialkot, for their hospitality during my stay in their village and in the Sind; Haji Abdul Shakur of Khaiderabad, district of Lyallpur; Chowdhri Nasrullah of Talwandi, district of Gujranwala, and his family; the late Pir Budhen Shah of Multan; Dr. and Mrs. A. Waheed of Lahore; Mrs. A. Kekaus of Lahore; Sheikh Akhtar Hussain of Gujrat and his mother; Chowdhri Jehan Khan of the village of Gumnana, *tahsil* of Phalia, district of Gujrat, and his family; and Chowdhri Muhammad Shafi of Parianwali.

To all the people of the place where the anthropologist has carried on his work, a debt of gratitude is owed which cannot well be expressed in words, for these are his collaborators whose frankness and trust open doors to a new world. Chowdhri Fazl Ahmad of Mohla, district of Gujrat, and his family did indeed open the doors of their house to me. Their kindness and generosity made it possible for me to remain for a prolonged period in the Punjab and to carry on my work. Their friendship made this a rich experience in my life. The insight which Chowdhri Fazl Ahmad has into the ways of his people and his comprehension of the task of an anthropologist have been my steady guides to an understanding of the people of Mohla and of the Punjab. I have to thank him also for the diagrams which he prepared for my use in this study.

The village people, with whom I spent so many hours and to whom I put so many difficult questions, were consistently kind, co-operative, and protective. Among them all, I shall especially remember Badro, the *tongawala*, whose carriage and whose joyful company were always at my disposal; Ghulam Muhammad, the loyal family servant of Chowdhri Fazl Ahmad; Nazir-nai, the barber of the village; Muhammad Hussain, the cobbler of the village, who gave me insight into the spiritual life of the people; Lal Khan, the *paṭwari*, who represented for me the worldly side of a Punjabi man; and Akbar, the former *paṭwari*, who became a *fakir* and was in search of the true path.

I wish to thank Mr. S. M. Ikram, Visiting Professor of Pakistan Studies, Columbia University, 1957–1958, for his kindness in reading this manuscript. For his assistance in working out the transliterations of Punjabi terms used in this study, I have to thank Dr. Theodore Schwartz. I wish also to thank Dr. Rhoda Métraux for her help and advice in my work.

ZEKIYE EGLAR

Cambridge, Massachusetts
August 1, 1959

PUBLIC DISPLAY OF DOWRY

In center foreground a village bard is describing the various articles in the dowry

Contents

Illustrations

Prologue: The Wider Setting

Pakistan covers two areas, in the northwest and northeast of the subcontinent of India, separated from each other by a thousand miles of alien territory. The two sections are called West Pakistan and East Pakistan and are often referred to as the West and East wings. This unique location came about as the result of the creation of Pakistan as a separate state for the Muslims of India and of the allocation to the state of those areas in which Muslims were in the majority.

West Pakistan includes the provinces of Sind, Baluchistan, the North-West Frontier Province, and Punjab,[1] and the former princely states which were joined to Pakistan after the Partition. Up to 1955, these provinces had a semiautonomous status; each had a provincial capital and an administrative and a legislative body. Then by a decree of October 14, 1955, they were merged into one unit, West Pakistan, of which Lahore, formerly the provincial capital of Punjab, became the capital.

Among the western provinces, the old province of Punjab is the

[1] At the time of the Partition, in 1947, the old province of Punjab was divided between India and Pakistan. At first the portion of the province which became part of Pakistan was called West Punjab to distinguish it from East Punjab, which became part of India. Later the government of Pakistan decided that West Punjab was to be known simply as Punjab. In this study, when the period preceding the Partition is being discussed the word Punjab refers to the whole province. For the period following the Partition, either Punjab or West Punjab is used to designate that portion of the old province which is now included in Pakistan.

best known. It has been settled longer than the others and has been the crossroad of many invasions. Lahore was the seat of rulers and, for a long period, was a center of culture and learning. The British annexed the Punjab to their other possessions in India in 1849, after they had defeated the last Sikh ruler. Before the coming of the British, there had been a period of great unrest, for the Sikh dynasty, which had built up a strong kingdom in the northwest and had ruled Punjab in the nineteenth century, had weakened, and the country was in turmoil until the British reestablished peace and order.

As in Bengal and other parts of India, the British used land-ownership as a basis for organization and as a means of systematizing and facilitating the collection of revenues. In 1857, the Regular Settlement was made which gave permanent ownership to those families who were already in possession of land. One effect of the Act was to make the holding of land the privilege of a single caste, the *zamindars,* who then became responsible for the payment of taxes to the government, not in crops but in cash. In this connection, land was divided into various categories according to which revenues were fixed. The necessity to deal with land problems and to arrange for the payment of taxes gradually brought about increased contact between the *zamindars* and the government outside the villages where they lived.

For purposes of better administration and communication, the British built new roads and improved old ones to make them usable throughout the year. The construction of railroads also was begun in the middle of the nineteenth century; by 1863 there were 4,000 miles of railroads crisscrossing the countryside. The completion of the Suez Canal in 1869 and the building of large steamships further facilitated the transport of raw materials from India and the import of manufactured goods from England. So, slowly, the Punjabi villages, which during the centuries of Mogul and Sikh rule had remained self-sufficient, came out of their isolation. As crops could be sold for cash and as their sale was no longer restricted to local

areas, landowners gradually moved toward a cash crop economy and money circulated more freely in the villages.

The great possibilities of the Punjab as an agricultural area were recognized by the British. Dams and irrigation canals were constructed and, beginning in 1892, vast tracts of new land became available for cultivation. The opening of the new colonies meant, on the one hand, the extension of village society, but also, on the other hand, a loosening of traditional ties as colonists from the old established villages moved out and took up land in the new ones. People did not break their ties with their kin; they even kept possession of their old land and strengthened old ties through new marriages and frequent visiting back and forth. Yet the sphere of their significant activity broadened very considerably, for in order to visit, and to take part in family celebrations, they had to travel not to the next village but many miles by train or, later, by bus.

Gradually, as these changes were taking place, village people became aware of and increasingly dependent upon goods and services coming from outside their local world. However, not all villages were affected to the same degree in such matters as cultivating cash crops, buying machine-made goods, or entering into new types of activities and new forms of relationships. Depending on their location and the size of landholdings, villages in the part of the Punjab which had long been settled—those, for instance, in the districts of Gujrat, Gujranwala, and Sialkot, where land was not abundant and was held in relatively small parcels—were less rapidly affected by change than were the new colonies of Sargodha, Lyallpur, or Montgomery with their vast tracts of land and more advanced methods of irrigation.

Acquaintance with manufactured goods, their increasing availability, and the increasing availability of money, together with some contact with city life, affected the kinds of work done by craftsmen in the villages—some craftsmen more than others—and the ideas and demands of village people as a whole. These changes in turn contributed to further changes in village life.

Awareness of a mode of life different from the traditional one appears to have increased during the First World War, when men from the villages were recruited into the army and were sent abroad to various parts of the world. Their families at home received their salaries and, as people became increasingly short of working hands, they became increasingly dependent upon money and on products which could be bought instead of being made at home. Meanwhile, the men who went abroad became acquainted with many foreign things. So, for instance, tea was introduced into the villages by the returning soldiers, and nowadays tea with milk is a favorite drink among the villagers.

Changes of the same kind took place on a larger scale during the Second World War. Again, many men were recruited into the army and served abroad. At home the prices of agricultural products rose, and money became more available in the villages. In addition, in this period, village people became more politically conscious. Until then, although they knew about the period of Sikh rule and the coming of the British Raj, the events of the transfer of rule from one ruler to another meant little more to them than episodes in a story. Now, however, members of political parties held rallies, and people who went to the cities would bring back news, including political news. In the city mosque after the Friday prayer there were political discussions, and people went to the city specially to attend them.

Gradually, as other changes took place, some people moved out of the villages to the cities and there adopted a somewhat different way of life. Their sons received new types of education and entered new occupations. But these changes were not always immediately apparent to those who remained in the villages. In the first place, those who left, as individuals, often kept their families in the villages where they maintained traditional relationships. Secondly, those who moved their families still kept their land and their connections with village people and remained familiar with village ways. So, as far as the village people were concerned, the basic

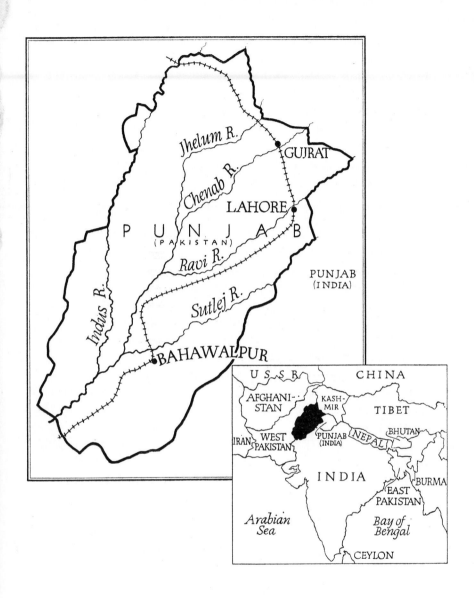

MAP 1. THE PUNJAB, PAKISTAN, AND SURROUNDING AREA

principles of social relationships and the modes of behavior through which they were expressed were little disturbed.

During the period of a hundred years after the annexation of Punjab by the British, change was continuous, but the rate of change was slow enough so that villagers of each generation could adapt themselves to the new without feeling that their lives were profoundly affected. And, in fact, traditional social relationships remained very stable. So, for the villagers, the implications of the changes taking place in the larger world became apparent only in recent years, particularly in the years since the establishment of Pakistan as an independent state. Then, among other changes, two occurred which were of immediate importance to the village people.

The first had to do with the land. In the Objective Resolution passed by the Constituent Assembly of Pakistan, March 12, 1949, the following statement is made:

> In the name of Allah, the Beneficent, the Merciful;
>
> Whereas sovereignty over the entire Universe belongs to Allah Almighty alone, and the authority which he has delegated to the State of Pakistan through its people for being exercised within the limits prescribed by Him is a sacred trust . . .
>
> Wherein shall be guaranteed fundamental rights including *equality of status, of opportunity.* . . .[2]

Translated into practical terms, the rights of "equality of status, of opportunity" meant—among other things—land reform. The size of landholdings was restricted and the right to purchase land was extended to all men alike instead of being limited to the members of one group alone.

The second change had to do with inheritance and was initiated by the West Punjab Muslim Personal Law (Shariat) Application Act of 1948, which was enacted by the provincial legislature of West Punjab. This Act gave—among other things—full rights of inheritance, particularly of agricultural land and other property, to

[2] Quoted in *Report of the Basic Principles Committee* (as adopted by the Constituent Assembly of Pakistan, September 21, 1954), p. 1 (italics mine),

women who, heretofore, had received dowries but had been excluded from the inheritance of property, which descended exclusively in the male line.[3]

These new rights, incorporated into law, touch upon two of the most important social relationships in village life—the relationship between landowners and nonlandowning craftsmen and that between a married woman and her parents' house. For the first time, change has penetrated to the core of social life. What the effect will be, however, remains to be seen.

This book describes the life of village people in Punjab at the moment of change. West Punjab has an area of 62,245 square miles and a population, according to the census of 1951, of some eighteen million people. There are more than nineteen thousand villages in the province, and more than 82 percent of the people live in villages.

The villages of the Punjab have a very distinctive character. The houses, with the exception of a few large brick houses belonging to well-to-do landowners, are built of clay and all are flat-roofed. Each house is hidden behind high clay walls on which, here and there, dung cakes for fuel are left to dry in the sun. Every village, no matter how small, has its mosque. The narrow, irregular lanes, muddy during the rainy season and deep in dust at other times, often serve as channels through which dirty water flows from the houses. On the outskirts of the villages are ponds of rain water for

[3] In 1937, the Shariat Act made provision for the application of Muslim Personal Law (Shariat) to all Muslims in British India except for those in the North-West Frontier Province. However, succession to agricultural land was specifically excepted, for the Act read, in part:

"Notwithstanding any custom or usage to the contrary in all questions (save questions relating to agricultural land) . . . the rule of decision in cases where the parties are Muslim shall be the Muslim Personal Law (Shariat)." (See Asaf A. A. Fyzee, *Outlines of Muhammedan Law* [London, Oxford University Press, 1949], p. 407.)

The West Punjab Personal Law (Shariat) Application Act of 1948 dealt further with the same problem but applied especially to Punjab and made new provision for succession to land.

the buffalo. Wherever fields are irrigated by wells, Persian wheels are outlined against the sky. The day starts early with the call to prayer from the village mosque and ends at sunset. A few people have kerosene lamps and the rest burn oil in small tin lamps, but except on moonlit nights there is little movement outside the court-yards after dark. Paths connect the scattered villages but, though there is constant traffic between villages, few strangers are seen from one week to the next. Before an official leaves his office in the city to visit a village, the village headman or watchman will be notified that a visit is intended. Village people may travel far and wide but no outsider comes into the village unless he has something special to do there or wishes to visit someone he knows.

No two clusters of villages in the Punjab are exactly alike. Yet there is a village way of life, which is best understood through the lives of people in a particular village. So Mohla, the village in which I lived for over five years and which is described here, is both unique and, in its own way, typical of the Punjab.

Part I. The Village of Mohla

1

The Village

The village of Mohla is in the heart of the Gujrat district of the province of Punjab, seventy miles northwest of Lahore. It lies midway between the two district towns Wazirabad and Gujrat. To the east of the village the railroad tracks run parallel to the Grand Trunk Road which crosses the country from Lahore to Peshawar and the Khyber Pass in the northwest. To the southwest flows the Chenab River, which threatens the village with periodic floods.

From Lahore one travels to Mohla by train or bus in about three hours. As the train leaves the city, the domes of the famous Badshahi mosque can be seen glistening against the blue sky; nearby on raised ground is the Fort of Lahore, which was built by Mogul emperors. In a few minutes the train crosses the bridge over the Ravi River. Along the banks are palm trees and luscious vegetation. On one bank above a beautiful Mogul garden rise the minarets of the majestic tomb of Jehangir, a Mogul emperor; on the opposite bank, half hidden by trees in a small garden is the modest tomb of his beloved wife, Nur Jehan. The highway runs parallel to the railroad tracks. Buses, cars, trucks, bullock carts, *tongas*, and men traveling on foot—all move along this highway. Soon the rich vegetation disappears and the land takes on a barren appearance. In the rainy season the land turns marshy, but in other seasons it glistens with "white alkali." In this soil no crop grows except paddy. During the season of paddy, the fields are green and men are seen at work, but there are no villages in sight.

The train stops at one or two small stations. The first big station is Kamoke, seventeen miles from Lahore. It is a rice market and has a number of rice-husking mills. During the harvest season sacks of rice are piled in mountainous stacks in the storage yards near the station. Beyond Kamoke there is another stretch of barren land, but before the train reaches the next large station, Gujranwala, forty-two miles from Lahore, villages begin to appear near the road and fields stretch out into the distance. Gujranwala, which is a district headquarters, is a historic city, the former seat of Sikh rulers. Here, trains and buses stop for a few minutes. Vendors in the station sell aerated water, cold sweetened milk diluted with water, hot tea, sweet puffed rice, popcorn seasoned with hot spices, sweetmeats, and the fruits of the season. At the bus stop, in the hot season, there may be a man with a huge straw fan who, for a fee, will fan the passengers. At the railroad station bearers bring trays of food to the cars. In the morning they serve an English-style breakfast, but later in the day they bring Pakistani meals.

The next big station is Wazirabad. This is a junction from which tracks branch off to Sialkot, Lyallpur, and Gujrat. After leaving Wazirabad, the train crosses the long bridge over the Chenab River. Near one bank there is a large timber market, where the timber floated down from the regions near the Himalayas is collected. Farther off there is a forest reservation.

Now the road is lined by huge poplar trees. In ten minutes the train stops at the Kathala station, which is also a bus stop. Across the road to the east one can see the village of Kathala. To the west, beyond a stretch of barren land, the eye stops at a cluster of trees and mud walls—that is Mohla.

From the station it takes about twenty minutes to walk directly to Mohla. Baggage is left at the station master's office to be picked up later by the barber or some other craftsman from the village. If one arrives in the afternoon, the sun shines hard in his eyes as he walks toward the village. After crossing the railroad track and climbing down a steep embankment, one walks westward over uneven, barren terrain, crossing the narrow boundaries of the plowed fields, past the simple village graveyard, around the hollows dug out for mud used in building village houses, through more fields, reaching, finally, a well dug under a clump of trees. The well marks the end of a bumpy dirt road which connects Mohla with nearby villages to the south and also leads to the main road and the railroad tracks—a much longer and more roundabout way of coming from the station to the village by horse and carriage.

Mohla has a population of approximately 350. If one includes the people of the neighboring villages, between which there is constant coming and going and whose fields merge, there are over 1,500 in the local population.

Like all villages in the Punjab, Mohla lies on an open plain where nothing cuts across the vastness of the sky and the earth as they meet at the horizon. Villages lie ahead and to all sides of Mohla, all of them alike in the color that predominates—the reddish gray color of the soil, the clay one treads on, the fallow fields, and the mud walls that protect from view the flat-roofed mud houses.

Punjab is an agricultural province. Its vast plains are covered with an intricate network of villages lying at distances of a quarter of a mile to two miles from each other. Over 82 percent of the people live in villages, which vary in size of population from 200 to 5,000, but which in physical appearance, average landholdings, economic and social structure, and in the pattern of daily living vary so little that all are equally representative of rural Punjab.

In fact, there is no large gap between village and city life. Most city people still maintain close connections with the villagers. They own land in the villages and have relatives there; for the sake of prestige they maintain a house in the village, too. On big occasions they either come to the village to celebrate or else invite their relatives to come to the city to participate in the event and also call upon some of the village craftsmen who are traditionally attached to their family to help at the ceremony.

The villages lie in clusters of three or four. As a result of the spread of landholdings, many villages have offshoots which are named after the original villages. Gurali (meaning Little Gurala) is an offshoot of Gurala, and there are Samañ and Lenda (West) Samañ, Dhirke and Nikke (Little) Dhirke, Mohla and Lenda (West) Mohla, and so forth.

Within the boundaries of its own lands, each village site is drawn close to a place of some advantage to it—a dirt road, a railroad track, a nearby city or a market town, a piece of high ground offering protection from the floods, a source of drinking water in an arid area, or another village whose nearness gives a feeling of safety. In this way, several villages form a cluster, in which each is separated from the others only by a few fields, with the rest of the village lands stretching beyond the village sites. At distances of twenty or thirty miles the points of orientation of the villages may change, but there are few differences in the style of village life. All these villages are connected by dirt roads, but the people use the boundaries of the fields for shortcuts. The dirt roads between the villages in turn join the metaled roads that lead into the bigger towns and cities or reach the Grand Trunk Road that parallels the main railroad track. Not a village is isolated and, except in time of flood, all can be reached by car, by horse and carriage, on horseback, or on foot.

Sometimes there are very specific ties between villages. Mohla, for instance, has a very close relationship to Dhirke, one and a half miles away. In the first place, Mohla is settled on land which originally belonged to Dhirke. Fifty years ago, Mohla and its lands were located near the Chenab River, but the whole village was washed away and most of its land was submerged. At that time, the then leading landowner of Mohla and some members of his patrilineage bought some barren ground from Dhirke, and founded the present Mohla. The fact that Mohla bought land from Dhirke does not add to the amount of land shown in the land records as belonging to Mohla. The purchase or sale of land by a village does not alter the size of the land originally allotted to each village by the Regular

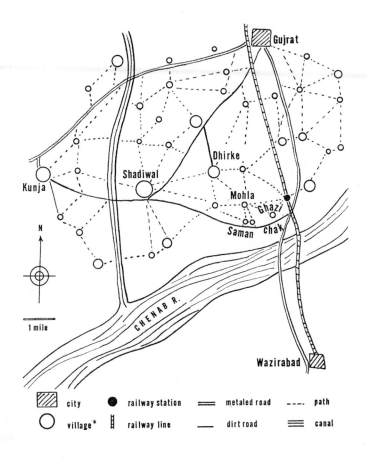

MAP 2. MOHLA AND SURROUNDING VILLAGES

* Size of circle indicates population which ranges here from 200 to 5,000.

Settlement in 1857. Therefore, in the Land Record Office, the land bought by Mohla is still on the records of Dhirke but the names of the new owners have been substituted for the old ones. The *lamberdar* of Dhirke, the revenue head of the village, collects from the owners in Mohla the revenues from the lands purchased from Dhirke.

Now that the lands of Mohla and Dhirke are contiguous, this very fact establishes between the people of these two villages a relationship to which they refer as being *bane da bhai*, brothers by having a common boundary. Besides, at the time of settlement, some people from Dhirke, whose lands were closer to Mohla than to Dhirke, came and settled in Mohla.

The people of these two villages borrow grain and money and buy cattle on credit from each other. People prefer to buy a buffalo or cattle in a village with which they have an established relationship. In the first place, they can buy on credit, and, secondly, they feel more confident that they will not be cheated; if they are dissatisfied, some adjustment will be made.

So, for instance, a man from Dhirke bought a buffalo from the carpenter in Mohla. They agreed on a price, which was to be paid later. After the buffalo was taken to Dhirke, it did not thrive. Within a few days it could hardly stand, ceased to give milk, and finally died. The new owner came back to Mohla, bringing with him a landowner who was married to a girl from Mohla. A few responsible men from Mohla and the neighboring village of Samañ came together. The man who had bought the buffalo claimed that it must have been sick at the time of the purchase, but that the carpenter did not tell him so; consequently he refused to pay. The main point of the long discussion that followed was whether the carpenter knew that he was selling a sick animal; finally, he admitted it was so. It was then decided that the man from Dhirke should pay half the price of the buffalo, because he also should have used his judgment at the time of the purchase. All the parties concerned were satisfied with the decision.

People from Mohla buy *ghi,* eggs, and chickens from Dhirke when there is a shortage in Mohla. If there is a need for collective labor, *mang,* during the harvest or the ploughing season, they ask for help through their relatives or friends. On the occasion of a marriage, they also ask for bedding, cots, copperware, and milk. In Dhirke there lives a *hakeem,* a native doctor, and the people from the neighboring villages go there to consult him. When a person of one village dies or loses a buffalo or suffers some other material loss, people of the other village go in groups to offer their sympathy.

The same pattern of relationships exists with the other villages near Mohla. With some they share a common carpenter, tailor, and blacksmith. A washerman from Nikke Dhirke washes the laundry from Mohla and Samañ. There are three small shops in Mohla run by a widowed weaver woman, a baker's wife, and the village *imam,* the priest. But certain things are found in Samañ shops; for example, people go there to buy dyes for cloth and native medicine. They also borrow agricultural implements from Samañ. In Samañ lives a *pir,* a religious man, to whom people go for faith curing. There is also a holy pool there, where childless women from all over the district come to bathe and are believed to be cured. Samañ holds annual *melas,* festivals held to commemorate the anniversary of the death of a holy person or a ruler, attended by the villagers—mostly men and children—from the neighborhood.

During the month of *Muharram,* which is the first month of the Muslim calendar, a *pir* from Gujrat is invited to Mohla to preach a sermon, and from all the neighboring villages come men, women, and children to listen. The primary school in Mohla—opened by the government in 1953—which has an enrollment of about 100 children, serves the five villages in the immediate vicinity. The headmaster, a weaver by caste, lives in the village of Samañ, about an eighth of a mile away; his father, with whom he lives, is the *imam* of a mosque in the village of Kathala, across the railroad tracks.

Every day, from Samañ and the village next to it, Ghazi Chak, the women vegetable growers, the *arains,* bring fresh vegetables to Mohla and the other villages. A man from Mohla collects milk in the neighboring villages and sells it in the city.

Men from these villages are invited to participate in the village *parea,* the village council. If there is something to be done in connection with the government, such as getting a fishing license or producing a birth certificate for marriage or inheritance, with obtaining a concession on excise taxes, when, for example, a crop like tobacco has spoiled, or with the court, people would find someone, through friends, who has good connections and would ask him to accompany them and to use his influence. This is never refused. There is coming and going between the villages all the time. On warm moonlit nights, men come to visit and they stay on until late in the night.

There are five girls from Dhirke married in Mohla, and three girls from Mohla married in Dhirke. Marriage ties establish close relationships between the villages, because daughters come home for regular visits, and on big occasions the people related through marriage come together. The village respects its daughters and respects the place where they are married. But though there are marriages between the nearby villages, the proximity of a village is not a basic factor in making a marriage connection. People often say that it is better not to marry a daughter into a nearby village, for there will be too much gossip traveling back and forth.

Sometimes there are quarrels between neighboring villages, which may be settled between themselves or through the intervention of an influential man from another village. Repeated straying of cattle into the fields of another village, an illicit relationship, or an elopement may lead to an outburst of anger and even to fighting. When, for instance, the daughter of a carpenter in Dhirke eloped with a blacksmith of West Mohla, the carpenter and his relatives repeatedly asked for the return of the girl. But the blacksmith did not heed them, nor did his village force him to do so. Finally, the men of Dhirke sent a warning that they were coming to beat up the men of West Mohla and to carry away one of the women of the blacksmith's family—either his sister or the wife of his brother. Frightened, because Dhirke is a large village, the people of West Mohla sent for the *chowdhri,* the most influential landowner, of Mohla proper. From Dhirke came a crowd of about 100 men armed with heavy clubs. The *chowdhri* of Mohla, whose mother was from Dhirke and who had good connections with that village, asked the crowd from Dhirke to send representatives with whom he and other landowners from West Mohla could hold a discussion. To this meeting the brother of the blacksmith was summoned. He was forced to promise that the girl would be returned within a specified number of days. As a guarantee he had to deposit with a responsible landowner of the village golden ornaments worth 400 rupees, which belonged to his wife. The carpenter's daughter was returned. A few months later she was married in the proper way to the blacksmith with whom she had previously eloped. (It may be remarked here that although there is no intermarriage between the different castes, carpenter and blacksmith are considered to be close enough for marriage.)

In this network of villages there are *kasbas,* larger villages, with bazaars, where one can buy cloth, shoes, cigarettes, fruit, meat, sweetmeats, and many other native products, as well as a few items from the outside. There also are found specialized craftsmen, such as goldsmiths.

People also go to the nearby cities of Gujrat and Wazirabad, each of which is five miles away from Mohla. Gujrat is the district headquarters; it has a civil hospital, offices of the Departments of Agriculture and Education, a cooperative bank, textile, pottery and furniture industries, an extensive bazaar, and a grain market. People prefer to go to Gujrat to buy provisions and cloth, for it has the larger bazaar. However, whenever the village barber goes to visit his aunt in Gujranwala, a city twenty-four miles away toward Lahore, he is asked to bring back brassware and to buy or to inquire about the price of cloth and of *lungis,* wrap-arounds, for this city is

19988

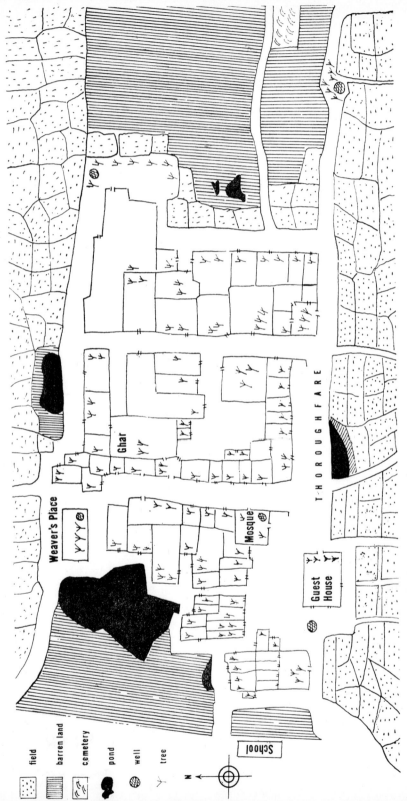

MAP 3. THE VILLAGE OF MOHLA

Weaver's Place

Ghar

Mosque

Guest House

THOROUGHFARE

School

field
barren land
cemetery
pond
well
tree

N

known for its brassware and for the *lungis* made in its vicinity. To
buy cloth in quantity, when it is needed for a marriage, for instance, people may go either to Gujrat or to one of the larger cities
where they can choose from a greater selection; where they go depends on where they have relatives with whom they can stay and
who will help them to find their way successfully. So, just as the
people who live in the cities still keep their places in the village
network, the village people, depending upon the same ties, feel
free to stay with their relatives in the city and to avail themselves
of their advice and help.

In the province of Punjab, there are two main types of villages:
the old villages, which have been built and rebuilt without any
apparent plan, except that, for protection, the back walls of the
houses are joined together, and the newer villages in the colonies
which have opened since 1887, in which wide streets divide the
village into regular blocks, each having a few houses with spacious
courtyards and all surrounded by high mud walls. The village of
Mohla belongs to the old type of Punjabi village.

The larger portion of Mohla lies to one side of the country road
—the main thoroughfare that runs in an east-west direction and
leads to the villages beyond. A few narrow lanes branching from
the main road cut the village into compact irregular blocks.

Across the main country road, all by itself, stands a brick building
with an arcaded veranda and four slender tall trees in front of its
wide compound which is surrounded by a low brick wall. This is
the men's guest house. Behind it is a Persian wheel drawn by
buffaloes, and beyond is a small block of mud houses, a new offshoot of the village, the place where people have had to move for
lack of space on the raised ground of the main site.

There are two or three vacant plots in the village, which are used
as shortcuts for crossing from one block to another and sometimes
for tethering buffaloes. These belong to landowners who have
moved to the new colonies where they have acquired land. Though

they have moved away, they keep the land in their name and may, sometime in the future, build a house there, for this is their original village from which they have not severed their ties, and here, in this village, are their relatives.

A few ponds of standing water are scattered on the outskirts of the village—some for the buffaloes to swim in and to drink from, others too shallow to be used by the animals yet too large to dry up.

And all round are the fields, some belonging to the neighboring village and merging into the boundaries of Mohla. The fields of Mohla stretch to the north and the southwest where the Chenab River flows—the river that has claimed many fields and has left many a landowner without land, but with the hope that the land may emerge some day, as has happened before and will no doubt happen again, for the river has its own cycle.

II

The Compound

In Mohla the houses in each of the irregular village blocks are built with their back walls joined together as a protection against thieves and floods. In front each opens onto a courtyard surrounded by a high wall that demarcates the household boundary and gives the house dwellers privacy from the world outside. The most spacious of the courtyards are forty by fifty feet, the smallest twenty by twenty feet.

The houses have no special orientation. The direction in which each house faces depends on two factors: the necessity felt to build so that no back wall is ever exposed and the position on the block. Thus, if one moves around one of the village blocks which is bounded by the main road on the south, by lanes on the west and the north, and by a narrow path on the east, it will be found that the houses face in the four directions—out toward the streets.

The houses of the richer landowners and some of the more well-to-do craftsmen are built of baked brick; the rest are made of mud. The better houses have covered verandas which run the length of the front of the house. Otherwise the plan of each house is similar. The houses are rectangular in shape, with one long room in front and two rooms at the rear. The back rooms have no windows and open into the front room. The front room may have windows—with wooden shutters but no panes of glass—that open onto the veranda; most houses, however, have no windows at all.

One of the back rooms serves as a storeroom for provisions. These are kept in earthenware and brass vessels of varying sizes, piled on top of one another with the largest vessel at the bottom and the smallest at the top. Sugar, *ghi,* flour for immediate use, salt, lentils, peas, peppers, pickles, jam, and brown sugar are kept in these vessels which are stored with extra housewares. The second back room is used for storing extra bedding, which is kept in huge tin boxes or piled up on wooden stands. Here are also smaller tin boxes, each belonging to one of the female members of the family. In them they keep clothes. In poor families, extra bedding and clothes are kept in a big wooden box. The women also use this room for the night and early morning prayers on cold winter days. Money and jewelry are hidden away in the least expected places—in a hole, behind a loose brick in the wall, in a vessel with some provisions, or in a bin of grain.

In the front room stand the large clay bins which contain the yearly supply of grain for the family. Also in this room, high on the wall, is a shelf on which are displayed brass vessels, trays, plates, and glasses; the number of these, in addition to the number of extra cots and the amount of extra bedding, is a sign of the wealth of the family and its ability to entertain guests. A few wooden pegs are driven into the clay walls to hold the clothes that are being used. The front room serves as a sleeping room for all the members of the family, male and female. There is little furniture other than the cots, though there may be a small mirror used by the women and, except in the poorest homes, a wooden armchair and a small table for a very respected male guest. The wealthiest landowner has several wooden armchairs; however, the villagers themselves use these only in the men's guest house for persons of high status and as a special treat. Women prefer to sit on the string cots, which are used for a variety of purposes, or on low stools while they cook, spin, or weave long strips used for covering the cots.

The ceiling is made of heavy beams, which are the most expensive part of the house structure; the roof is plastered with clay. The floors of the rooms are plastered with a mixture of clay, dung, and straw, which is renewed annually; every week or so a thin slip of dung, clay, and water is pressed over as a finish.

The front room is used for sleeping during the cold months from December to the end of February, and also for resting in the hot afternoons in summer. As the weather grows warmer, people move out on the veranda to sleep, then pull the cots into the courtyard, and finally transfer them to the roof, which is reached from the courtyard by a mud staircase. During the warm rainy season, people sleep on the roof and come down only when it starts to rain hard, carrying their cots with the bedding on their heads.

All the daily work is done in the courtyard or on the veranda. Women move their cots and their work about in the courtyard, sitting in the sunshine in winter and looking for shade in summer. There is usually a tree in the courtyard, and people spend much time in its shadow.

Cooking is done in the courtyard in an open structure—a flat roof supported by a few columns with the wall of the compound as its back wall. Two or three clay hearths are built next to the columns. This is the regular kitchen; in addition, there are other hearths built in the different parts of the compound where, in winter, one gets more sunshine.

Also in the courtyard are the buffaloes, standing by their long clay mangers along one of the walls of the compound. There is a room in the compound where the cattle stand in winter. In summer it is used for storing hay, but toward winter, as the amount of hay decreases, space is made for the cattle. Chickens and crows intermingle everywhere; the crows, which visit the same houses year after year, are accepted as an inevitable part of the surroundings.

The people who live in one compound are closely related. They may form either a simple conjugal family consisting of a man, his wife, and children, or they may form a joint family consisting of an elderly father and mother, their married and unmarried sons, and unmarried daughters and sometimes a widowed daughter with her children. Such a joint family is considered to be a single household if the income is pooled and expenditures are made from a common purse. In this case, the parents—actually, most likely, the mother—manage the budget. When it comes to paying taxes, contributing to the village funds, or providing labor for communal work, such a household is treated as one unit, for, although there may be many grown-up men in the family, only one man will be required to contribute his work. However, when it comes to social dealings—as in *vartan bhanji,* the system of reciprocal gift exchange—matters are handled quite differently. If at the marriage of their sons, the parents have performed all the ceremonies which require the distribution of food in the village, these sons and their wives are entitled to be treated as if they had separate households; when other families in the village are distributing food or sweets, they will send to this compound sweets and rice for the parents and unmarried children, as one group, and for each of the married sons separately. On the other hand, as long as they spend from the common fund, the married sons themselves do not take part in the system of reciprocal gift giving. Rather, it is their parents who, on behalf of the whole family, conduct all the dealings on appropriate occasions and distribute food in the village.

After their sons have been married for some time, parents give the eldest son a separate room in their house or in the same compound and let him manage his own income and expenditures. From this time on, the eldest son is considered to have a separate household from every point of view—such as in paying taxes and contributing labor. And when it comes to *vartan bhanji,* he now takes an active part, celebrating important events, such as the birth or the circumcision of his son, and distributing food in the village. Whether he remains in the same compound or moves to a compound of his own, his is an independent household.

In contrast, a son whose marriage was not performed with the appropriate ceremonies, accompanied by the distribution of food in the village, is not recognized as a separate social entity but is still treated, in *vartan bhanji,* as a member of his parents' household. As long as he does not establish himself, he will remain so. His status will change only when he has a room of his own, cooks separately, and on the whole manages his own budget.

After the death of the parents, unmarried brothers and unmarried sisters live with one of the married brothers. Usually the married brothers live for some time together in the same compound; if the property was not divided during their parents' lifetime, they will continue as a joint household, for it is respectable to show unity. However, their wives may not get along well together, in which case the brothers would soon have separate cooking arrangements; later, when their children grow up, they will move to separate compounds. But the brothers will continue to work together.

When food is sent to a family who live together in one compound but who are divided into several households, people say that there are so many *chuls,* hearths, in that compound. In this case, *hearth* stands for cooking and symbolizes an independent household.

III

The Village Castes

There are two main castes in the village: *zamindar* and *kammi*. *Zamindars* are the landowners, and *kammis* are the village crafts-men.[1]

Zamindars differ in their social status in accordance with the size of their landholdings. The largest landholding is about seventy acres and the smallest about one and a half acre. Although some *zamindars*, as a result of the subdivision of land through inheritance, own hardly any land at all, the fact that at some time in the past their ancestors did own land makes them still belong to the *zamindar* caste. *Kammis* do not own land.[2] However, there are a few exceptions. A *kammi* may receive land as a gift from a *zamindar*, and once he owns the land it will be inherited by his descendants. For example, a very generous *zamindar* of Dhirke gave six acres of land to the father of the present blacksmith of the village Samañ, who had exceptionally pleased him with his work. Sometimes a *kammi* can purchase land if he can show that some ancestor of his up to the seventh generation owned a piece of land. In this way Babu Imam-Din of Samañ acquired land. He is a barber by caste, but is called *babu* because he has some education and is a clerk in

[1] For reasons of convenience, Punjabi terms used in this study are pluralized by adding *s*. Thus, the plural of *zamindar* is made *zamindars*.

[2] The Land Alienation Act of 1901, forbade the purchase of land by anyone who was not an agriculturalist, even by those who belonged to the business community. With the establishment of Pakistan in 1947, nonagriculturalists were permitted to purchase land. However, the mere fact of owning land does not make a *zamindar* of a *kammi*.

the railway engineering department. With very minor exceptions, then, it is the *zamindars* who are the only landowners.

Kammis are themselves divided into castes, such as barber, baker, potter, carpenter, which indicate the craft which they have inherited from their ancestors and which will be practiced by their sons. A child learns the caste it belongs to from the time it begins to speak, and tells it when he gives his personal name. Very early, the child also learns that it can marry only within its own caste. Yet the fact of belonging to different castes does not create social barriers among the people, all of whom are Muslims. *Kammis* and *zamindars* sit together and may eat together, accept food from one another's houses, smoke a common *huka*, draw water from a common well, and pray side by side. The fact of being Muslims creates a sense of unity and of equality among the people. In their eyes, caste is a custom which they have borrowed from the Hindus and which, to them, refers primarily to an inherited occupation. When a mature person is asked about his *zat*, which means caste and also identity, he is most likely to answer: "What identity can a human being have? The only one who has an identity is the Almighty. I am a carpenter (or *zamindar*, or barber, or this, or that) by occupation."

At the head of the village there is a *chowdhri*, the village chieftain or headman. He is of the *zamindar* caste. The title of *chowdhri* is an honorary one, and every *zamindar* is addressed as *chowdhri*, but there is a difference between one who is a *chowdhri* in name only and the actual *chowdhri* who is the head of the village. For this man has inherited his position from his father, whose ancestors were the founders of the village and had more land than the other *zamindars* and commanded respect and had influence through their wealth, generosity, common sense, and power. To hold onto his position, the *chowdhri* must have the qualities of a leader: he should have authority; he must be generous with his time and money; he should get along well with his *biraderis*, the members of his patrilineage, for on their unity depends his power; he must have many friends, maintain good relationships with the people, and have connections in official circles; he should act in every situation in accordance with his status, that is, he should be dignified and should be able to make decisions.

In a large village there is more than one such *chowdhri*, each backed by a group of followers—smaller *zamindars* and *kammis*—whom he favors and who form his party in the struggle for power with other parties in the village. But in a small village like Mohla there is usually only one *chowdhri*.

As a symbol of his status the *chowdhri* maintains a guest house, where his male guests are entertained. It serves also as a men's club for the people of the village, where the *huka* is served at any time, and where the men can exchange news, gossip, play cards, or lounge on the cots. Official guests from the city are received here, and here in the courtyard the *parea*, the village council, meets. Here a traveler may spend the night and be treated to a meal. Here the villagers may entertain their *barat*, wedding parties. And a man in whose family a death has occurred will spread straw mats on the ground in the courtyard to receive the friends and neighbors who for days come to offer condolences and to sit with him for a long time to show their sympathy for his grief.

Women do not use the guest house; they feel "ashamed." The wife of a *musalli*, a laborer, sweeps the courtyard at a time when the men are not around but even then she does not feel at ease. But the women in the *chowdhri's* household like to bring their women visitors to show them around when the men are away, for they take pride in the guest house, which is a symbol of the high status and generosity of the *chowdhri*.

The *chowdhri's* generosity must be supported and shared by his womenfolk—by his *ghar*, his household—because in this society a woman's cooperation, especially that of the *chowdhrani*, the *chowdhri's* mother or his wife, is crucial in building up and sustaining the prestige of the man. For women control all the provisions and the money. When a man has guests, it is up to the women what quality and what amount of food will be served and how good will be the bedding they will send, all of which indicate the status of the host. So a man has to maintain good relationships with the womenfolk of the house in order to have their good will.

Besides, the women should get along well among themselves, for should they fight, they would expose themselves to criticism and the *chowdhri's* prestige would suffer. How could he give advice to other people if there were no unity in his own household?

As the *chowdhri* has tenants to till his land, he has time to devote to village affairs. He forms a link between the people and the government. He sees to it that in times of distress his village gets a government loan, or, if there are any benefits to be enjoyed, he does not allow his village to be by-passed. When someone in the village gets involved in court or when anyone is in trouble, he uses his connections and influence to help them. In cases of theft, elopement, or dispute in the village, he calls together the *parea,* the village council; the matter is discussed and a decision is made by the *parea*—but the *chowdhri's* decision is final and carries weight. The *parea* has no connection with the government, and its composition depends upon the particular case to be put before it. Usually a few respectable *zamindars* and *kammis* of the village take part in it, and often one or two *zamindars* from the neighboring villages, who are known for their shrewdness and sound judgment and who are on friendly terms with the *chowdhri,* are also invited.

The women in the *chowdhri's* household—in Mohla, his mother or, in her absence, the widow of his elder brother—are the ones to whom people turn in time of need, whether the occasion is a joyful or a sorrowful one. They borrow from the *ghar*—the household of the *chowdhri*[3]—money and provisions and also get free medicine. Neighbors or *kammis* who have no buffalo, or whose buffalo goes dry, get their *lasi,* buttermilk, regularly from this house. When a child is born, *kammis* expect to get its first shirt from the *ghar,* for

[3] *Ghar* means house or household; in Mohla *ghar* refers to the household of the *chowdhri.*

it brings good luck. And when the poor die, the *chowdhrani* sees to it that they have a shroud.

On all important occasions in the houses of the *kammis*, the *chowdhrani* honors them by her presence. She gives the traditional money, the *selami*, to the bride or the bridegroom. When there is a death in the village or in one of the neighboring villages, she goes, heading a party of women, to offer condolences and her presence will enhance the importance of the event.

Likewise, whenever there is an important event in the *chow-dhri's* household, both the *kammis* and the *zamindars* of the village and their womenfolk show their attachment and loyalty by partici-pating in the celebration to the degree that is appropriate to their status and their closeness to the *chowdhri's* family. Other *zamindar* families in the village, in accordance with their status, have their own circle of *kammis* whom they favor.

In every village there are the following castes of *kammis:* barber, baker, cobbler, carpenter, potter, blacksmith, *musalli* (laborer), weaver, and tailor. Most villages have a *mirasi*, a village bard, and in some villages there are the castes of Kashmiri and of *araiñ*, the vegetable growers. The *araiñs* may own the land on which they cultivate vegetables, but they are not considered to be *zamindars*.

In a village the work of the *kammis* meets the basic needs of the community. Every *zamindar* family has a contract with a family of each of the following *kammis:* barber, baker, cobbler, carpenter, potter, blacksmith, washerman-tailor, and *musalli*. This contract is called *seyp*, and the contracting parties are *seypi* to each other. This set of *kammis* is referred to as *ghar da kammi*, that is, the *kammis* of the household. These *kammis*, besides rendering their specialized services to the household, have specific functions on all ceremonial occasions of the household of their *seypi*. *Kammis* also have con-tracts among themselves. Thus, a potter's household would have a *seyp* with a barber, carpenter, baker, and a *musalli*.

The work done by these *kammis* is defined by custom and usage. The barber, although he does do barbering, is also an official cook.

He cooks on all ceremonial occasions and also whenever the families with whom he has *seyp* have guests. He is the confidant of his *seypis* and is consulted about various important problems—especially those concerning marriage. He is a matchmaker, and through his connections with the barbers in distant villages he is able to find suitable spouses for his clients' children. He is also a messenger and takes important messages to families who may live as far as 150 miles away. The letters he carries say very little; the most important part of the message is transmitted orally. The barber is a receptionist and acts in this capacity at the guest house of the *chowdhri*. He prepares the *huka* for the guests and gives them the information they ask for. He massages[4] the guests of the *chowdhri* and serves them food. He also massages the *chowdhri*.

While the barber attends to his varied duties, the women of his household do the work which is complementary to his activities. His wife, for instance, is the hairdresser of the women in the household of the *chowdhri*. She also accompanies the women of the *chowdhri's* household whenever they go on visits, attend some ceremony, or go shopping in the nearby city. She also does errands for her other *seypis*. Whenever food is distributed from the houses of her *seypi*, the barber's wife carries it to the other houses. She knows how to cook in the way it is done in rich houses, and whenever her clients have a few guests she is called to cook. But if there are many guests, it is the barber himself who does the cooking. She also massages the *chowdhrani*, and she entertains the ladies by bringing them news from the village and from the outside. When a daughter of her *seypi* is married, she accompanies the bride to the house of her parents-in-law.

Women of other *kammi* castes also help their men in the activities of their occupations. While a potter kneads the clay and shapes the vessels, his wife helps him paint them and collects dung from her

---

[4] In this type of massage the masseur or masseuse presses or very gently kneads the limbs or back of the person treated. Even small children may acquire this skill.

seypi for fuel in the kiln; later she distributes the wares among her clients. A *musalli* works in the fields of his *seypi,* while his wife sweeps their houses and courtyards and shapes the dung cakes to be used as fuel. A baker, who is called a fisherman, does not do the baking. He goes fishing and hunting for partridges and quail and supplies the fuel to heat the oven. It is his wife who bakes the bread and parches wheat, barley, gram, corn, and rice. A cobbler's wife embroiders the leather from which the cobbler sews the native shoes.

A woman's participation in his work enables a craftsman to fulfill the requirements of his profession. A baker or a barber could not practice his craft unless he married a woman of his own caste who from early childhood had acquired the skills necessary for that craft by being the daughter of a baker or a barber.

A case may well illustrate this point. A cobbler's wife disappeared from the village. Months later word came from a distant village that she was there with a barber with whom she had eloped. In that village, a *seypi* of the barber had guests, and this woman was called upon to cook. When the lady of the house noticed that the woman could not cook the special dishes, she asked her how it was possible for a woman of the caste of barbers not to know how to prepare the traditional dishes. The woman then had to confess that she belonged to the cobbler's and not to the barber's caste. Thus her whereabouts became known.

The barber is ranked as the most refined among the *kammis.* He is a worldly man who travels to distant villages and cities and meets people of high and low status. He must exercise great discretion with regard to personal matters entrusted to him by his *seypis* and their various relatives and friends and he acts accordingly. The special position of the barber does not mean that his caste is considered to be higher than that of the other *kammis.* However, there is a degree of importance attached to the work of the different *kammis.* Some of them—the barber among them—are essential to the functioning of the village. Whenever nonarable land is reclaimed and a new village is formed, *zamindars* who intend to settle there will certainly take with them a barber, a carpenter, and a cobbler as the men most needed in an agricultural community.

In many villages there are *mirasis,* who are village bards. They know the genealogies of the big *zamindars* of their villages and also the households into which the daughters and daughters' daughters of these *zamindars* have been married. They do all the work of the barbers except barbering. Some of them entertain guests by playing musical instruments and by singing, and all of them are very able entertainers who can tell stories and jokes and speak well.

The caste of Kashmiri, who are found in some villages, do not have any special profession. They tend goats, do weaving, work as butchers, as laborers, and as tradesmen.

Weavers spin thread and weave cloth and the cotton blankets which are much in demand. However, they are not considered *ghar da kammi,* for people do not make contracts with them.

A *seyp,* or contract, is a relationship established not merely between two individuals, but between two families who become *seypi* to each other.[5] Families can enter this relationship at any time, and women as well as men may enter such a contract in behalf of their families. Usually, *seyp* relationships between two families were established generations ago and have been inherited by the families of the respective *seypis.* For example, a certain *zamindar* family inherits a *seyp* with a set of families of *ghar da kammi,* whose forefathers had been the *seypis* of the ancestors of the *zamindar* family. Thus, the partnership in a *seyp* continues for generations. Although a barber of a certain generation may not satisfy his *seypi,* nevertheless the contract would not be broken nor would his *seypi* change to another barber. It is a matter of honor and dignity for both partners to maintain the long standing relationship. So the nature of the relationship between the *seypis* is not to be understood as a merely economic one in which services and payment are equated. It is

[5] For an outline of mutual responsibilities between *seypis,* see Appendix I, *Seyp:* Work and Payments.

his mules to transport clay and bricks for construction, brings grain and straw in from the fields, and carries rice and grain to the mills for husking and grinding. A carpenter, beside making new ploughs and keeping old ones in good repair and doing the woodwork which goes into making Persian wheels, makes cots and does the general carpentry work for the village. A baker sells fish and game in the town market and sometimes brings them to the village also; in addition, he transports straw and grain on his horses. Payment for these services is made in grain or money at the time that the work is done.

During the busy agricultural seasons, all the *kammis* in the village, except for barbers and *mirasis,* provide helping hands in the fields. At every stage of work—planting, cultivating, harvesting, and threshing the grain, and crushing the sugarcane—the *zamindar* needs some extra help. He can count on his *seypis* to work in his fields at least one day during each seasonal crop and pays for these services in grain at the time of the grain harvest. This grain is given in addition to what the *ghar da kammi* receive as *seypis.*

There are some occasions when the need for labor is particularly urgent, and to meet this need special arrangements are made. A *zamindar* may be under pressure of time to finish the work in his fields which may require numerous hands. This may happen at the time of ploughing, when the soil is drying out very rapidly or when the rains have been late so that there is little time left to plant, or it may be necessary to cut the crops in a hurry. On such occasions, a *zamindar* needs the help of many people and he sends word to the *zamindars* and *kammis* of his village and perhaps of neighboring villages for aid.

This work, which is done collectively for some person at his request, is known as *mang,* and the people who participate in such work are also called *mang.* In Punjabi, *mang* means "request," and the verb *mang·na* similarly means "to ask." When a group of men pass by carrying their working implements, people say that they look like a *mang.*

The task for which collective labor is called may or may not be completed in one day, but each person who comes works for one day only. The remaining work will be completed either by the person who asked for help or he may request others to contribute their labor.

Those who come to work as *mang* are not paid; their work is regarded as a favor done for the host. The host, in turn, feeds them twice, and the food provided must be plentiful and of good quality —usually including both a meat dish and a sweet. The meals are prepared by one of the village barbers with whom the *zamindar* has a *seyp*.

Mang may also be called for the sinking of a well. In many parts of Punjab, water for irrigation is obtained from wells, and most *zamindars* own wells or at least have a share in a well. For sinking a well, a *zamindar* engages three or four professionals, who are paid in money, but in addition the labor of seven or eight men is required for about a week. This labor is obtained by calling *mang*. Each *zamindar* and *kammi* who is invited to work contributes one day's labor. All those who come are, as usual, fed, and the host should on this occasion be especially lavish, for otherwise the well may not give water in abundance. Upon the completion of the well, sweets are distributed in the village and to those who come to visit the new well.

Roofing a house is another occasion for calling a *mang*. Usually the walls are built by the owner with the help of a laborer, but covering the roof with wet clay is a task that requires many hands because the layers of wet clay must be packed solid as quickly as possible before they dry out. For this reason, *mang* is called and the work is done in the afternoon when many people are available and the task can be completed in no more than two hours. After the roof has been covered, the owner of the house may pass a plate of brown sugar among the *mang*, each of whom will take a pinch. In this case, the man who has requested *mang* may be either a *kammi* or a *zamindar*, and both *kammis* and *zamindars* will take part in this work.

After a harvest, a *kammi* may have collected enough bushels of grain—some from his *seypis* and some through his work as a laborer in the fields—so that he needs help in threshing the grain. He may then request *mang*, as he needs the assistance of cultivators who own oxen and threshing boards. He treats them to a very good meal which is cooked by a barber.

Unlike *seyp*, collective labor is not a permanent arrangement in the village, nor does it stand for a binding relationship between two families. Yet it is an expression of the personal relationships existing within the village and beyond, and the significance of this relationship is not only economic but even more social and moral.

When a *zamindar* calls for *mang*, he is primarily under pressure of time at a period when everyone else is also very busy. Yet people respond by coming to help him. One may ask whether he could not, instead, have engaged laborers to complete his work and whether, by calling *mang*, there is some saving for him? It is difficult to find laborers during the busy season, since all of them are already working for various *zamindars*; secondly, a *zamindar* who invites *mang* is likely to spend as much, or even more, for the food he serves than he would have had he paid wages to laborers.

The importance of *mang* lies in the sphere of social relations. A *zamindar* who is able to assemble many people for a *mang* is one who has influence, has a wide circle of connections, and is much respected. For a *zamindar* to have his house built solely through *mang*, without the employment of any paid laborers, is a matter of great prestige and proof of the influence he has and the respect he commands in the community. Thus, a good response to his request for *mang* is an indication of the extensiveness of his social relationships. Besides, by calling people for the *mang*, he is testing the effectiveness of these relationships. The economic aspect of *mang*—the rapid completion of the work—is of secondary importance to him. Of much greater importance is strengthening the social bonds that exist between him and many members of the community. By calling people to work for him, he puts himself under obligation to all those who respond and opens the way for them, in turn, freely to ask favors of him. And this is his underlying objective: alternately to be obliged and to oblige, so that the scales of the relationship never come to a perfect balance. By keeping the scales in slight imbalance, he keeps these relationships active and alive; by a continuous check he is able to evaluate how he stands with these various people.

IV

Land and Prestige

Agriculture is the basis of Mohla's economy and land is the principal source of livelihood for all the people of this village. Yet arable land is a limited and much-valued possession. In Mohla, where there are twenty-six *zamindar* families, approximately one-third of the village people own land.

According to the records, the village of Mohla owns 1,092 acres of land, but approximately one-fourth of this land is under the river. However, Mohla has bought some land from Dhirke and other nearby villages. In 1857, by the Regular Settlement Act, the government allotted the original Mohla its 1,092 acres; part of this was arable land and the rest was pasturage. The first Mohla was washed away by flood, and the second Mohla was built on higher ground. Around the turn of the century, the second Mohla was also washed away, and almost all of its land was submerged. At that time many families left their native place, rented land in other villages, and became tenants. But some families remained. Among them, Nabi Bakhsh, the ancestor of the present *chowdhri* of Mohla, bought land from Dhirke. On this land was built Mohla proper, which exists today. At the time that Nabi Bakhsh bought the land, he distributed free plots for house sites among the *zamindars* and the *kammis* who did not go away. After some time, the river receded and some of the old land emerged. People who had left the former Mohla over twenty years before and who had settled in other villages began to return. Some settled in the village founded by Nabi Bakhsh while others settled half a mile away near their lands which had re-emerged, and in this way Lenda (West) Mohla came into being. Some of the people in Lenda Mohla built their houses on land belonging to Nabi Bakhsh, which they could have free. Others acquired land individually from Dhirke.

All these people in Mohla proper and in Lenda Mohla, who were given free house sites, do not own these plots, that is, they cannot sell them. But as long as they live in the village they have usufructuary rights which pass on to their children. Should they move away, they may sell the wood or whatever building material remains of their houses or, with the consent of the *chowdhri*, who is the owner, they may sell their houses without dismantling them, but with the understanding that the purchaser does not become the owner of the site on which a house stands. The village people cannot be evicted from their house sites; by virtue of having lived on a site for years and of having planted a tree, which everyone has in his courtyard, each family has full right of possession.

But this is not the case in all villages. In all the old villages, whoever settled there before or wishes to settle there now owns his house site, which he has purchased or will purchase from the *patti* —also called the *wand*—the section of the village in which the plot is located.

Nowadays, although the 1,092 acres which belonged to the original Mohla are still on the land records as belonging to the one village of Mohla, there actually are two villages, Mohla proper and Lenda Mohla. Of its total land, Mohla proper owns about half plus approximately 150 acres purchased from other villages. Some of this land is still submerged.

In spite of the fact that land is much valued, there are fields which lie fallow. Through subdivision by inheritance, one field may be the common property of several members of a *biraderi*, a patrilineage, none of whom will give up his share in favor of another even though the individual shares in the field are too minute to be cultivated. But used or unused, land is owned by the *zamindars*.

(In this chapter, problems of land ownership are discussed as they existed prior to the Partition and the institution of land reform.)

Though the ownership of land is the dividing line between *zamindars* and *kammis*, the interest of both is centered on the land. For the *zamindar*, it is important to make the land productive; to accomplish this, he needs the labor and the specialized services of the *kammis*. And the specialized crafts of the *kammis* are directly related to agriculture. Thus, the two groups are interdependent.

Exclusive ownership of land has given the *zamindars*, as a group, a position superior to that of the *kammis*, and land is the form of property for which the *kammis* have had the greatest longing.

Among the *zamindars* themselves, size of landholding is the basis on which social prestige is measured. A *zamindar* with large landholdings has more power, prestige, and influence, because he has more tenants and *kammis* who are attached to the land, work for him, and depend on him, than has a *zamindar* who has little land and, consequently, fewer tenants, or one who tills his own land. Having more land, a *zamindar* has more income, entertains more people, can make more connections, can extend his influence further into official circles, and therefore can help more people and command more respect; in this way he increasingly acquires power, influence, and prestige.

Social status based on ownership of land places on the *zamindar* certain responsibilities toward the people with whom he has established some relationship, as has already been mentioned. In particular, the generosity which the *zamindar* is expected to display is closely connected to other kinds of property, which should be distributed. "Flowing water becomes clean," is a proverb often quoted by the Punjabi, which means, of course, that one should not hoard property—that is, money or food—because through hoarding they become *mekru*, unclean. Rather, one should always distribute food and money; otherwise there will be no *barkat*, no abundance, in the house. The money will be spent on sickness; the cattle will die.

A *zamindar* distributes such property on every occasion: at the building of a house, the sinking of a well, the end of harvest, when a child is born, when a boy is circumcised, at times of sickness and convalescence, at a marriage, when an old person dies, and on the anniversary of the death of a person important in the family. On all such occasions, it is proper to distribute food, fruit, sweets, and money in the village, and each time a distribution takes place the *zamindar's izzet*—prestige, honor, and status—is increased. The more he gives, the more *izzet* he gains. As the Punjabi say, "One collects either property or *izzet*."

However, while his *izzet* is increased by the kind of property that represents income from the land, it is equally, or even to a greater degree, increased by the purchase of land which adds to the size of his holdings. Land itself is not a type of property which a *zamindar* would willingly part with. He may share food and money with others but not land, for this is the source of his *izzet*, and he identifies his land with his *pat, laj,* or *patlaj,* which, like *izzet,* are words referring to power, honor, influence, respect, prestige, and status.

Since to a *zamindar* land is the source of his power, he wants to keep it in his line. This strong feeling on the part of a *zamindar* for his land was recognized in and was well protected by the customary laws of inheritance. According to these laws, land remains in the male line—it is passed from father to son, none going to the daughters under normal circumstances. When a *zamindar* dies without leaving male issue, however, his daughters do inherit. If then a daughter leaves no issue, after her death the land is claimed by her father's brother, her father's brother's son, her father's father's brother's son, or indeed, it may be claimed by any male who can trace a connection in the male line to her father, that is, by any man who belongs to her father's *biraderi*, his patrilineage.

But an inheriting daughter who has sons passes land on to them. This land, inherited from the maternal line, is called *nanki virsa,* literally, property inherited from the mother's side. Men who inherit *nanki virsa* belong to a *biraderi* other than the one to which their mother's father belonged.

Customary law is concerned not only with inheritance of land, but also with its sale and purchase. In the village, the land belonging to the members of a *biraderi* is found in one *patti*, one section, of the village—all the separate holdings contiguous to each other, never scattered in two or more of the *patti* which form the village. A *zamindar* cannot sell his land at his own pleasure; rather, he must show some valid reason for doing so, such as the need to finance the education or marriage of his children or the wish to purchase another piece of land. Also his closest male kin have the first right to buy any such property: his brother, his brother's sons, his father's brother's sons, or else any other man in his *biraderi*, the closest kin having priority over the others. Only if no one in his *biraderi* is willing to buy the land can it be sold to another *zamindar* of the village; and only if no village purchaser is found can it be sold to an outsider.

These restrictions apply to *jedi virsa*, land inherited from ancestors in the male line. However, if a man wishes to sell land which he himself has previously acquired by purchase, he does not need to prove the necessity for the sale. But even then, where the sale of purchased land is involved, the *tahsildar*, the land revenue official, will make inquiries and will not confirm the sale unless it has been announced and the *biraderis* of the seller have had an opportunity to express any objections they may have. For just as a family wishes to keep its land within its own male line, so the *biraderis* want to keep the land owned by their various branches within the kin group. They do not want to have any strangers in their midst.

In almost every village there is an on-going struggle for power among the different *biraderis* of *zamindars* and often among the members of one *biraderi* as well. They have formed their own parties and have achieved some sort of balance of power in the village, and for this reason they feel that an outsider would take advantage of the struggle, would involve himself in village politics to gain power and prestige for himself, and thus would upset the existing balance.

However, this is not the only reason the *biraderis* resent outsiders. Every *zamindar* has a great attachment to and a deep feeling for his land, his *biraderi,* and his native village. Together with the ancestral land, he has inherited relationships with his *biraderi,* with the village people, and the neighborhood. These relationships have been built up through generations of interaction. And though there may have been ups and downs in these relationships—for there is always rivalry for power and prestige among the *biraderis,* one's own and the others in the village—nevertheless, to the *zamindar,* this is his own *biraderi,* or the *biraderi* of his village, and this is his own village. No newcomer, it is believed, can feel the same way about land acquired by purchase or as *nanki virsa.* Loyalty and attachment belong to a man's own *biraderi* and to his own paternal village.

The outsider who has purchased land may give it to a tenant, who may then cause great inconvenience to the *biraderi,* with whom he has no long standing relationships. Or, if the new purchaser settles in the village himself and if the property is large, in order to manage it he must engage labor among the *kammis* of the village. So he will attempt to gain power and influence quickly by unduly favoring the *kammis* and thus will spoil their relationships with the *zamindars* of the village which have existed for generations. Moreover, since he has no actual *biraderi* to support him in this village—for "*biraderi* is power"—in order to get a foothold and to feel secure, he will intrigue and will form a party of *kammis* and *zamindars* who have grievances against other *zamindars* or who want to exploit the situation; by so doing he will disrupt the existing organization of the village.

On the other hand, if he is not pleased with the *kammis* of this new village or prefers to favor the *kammis* of his native village, he may engage the latter to work on his newly purchased land, and by so doing deprive the *kammis* of this village of the work and income that is theirs by right. As almost every village is self-sufficient in the matter of labor, the introduction of *kammis* from another village may badly upset the village economy. Thus time and experience have proved to the *zamindars* the disadvantages of having an outsider come into their midst.

The Amir brothers inherited *nanki virsa* in the village of Jamke in the district of Gujranwala. It was a large property, and in order to manage it they needed influence and power. So they became involved in village politics, formed a party of their own, and fought with the other parties. In one such fight, a member of a local *biraderi* was murdered. This roused great antagonism, and it became very difficult for everyone to have them continue to live in the village.

Men who inherit *nanki virsa* may, instead of trying to form a party of their own, attempt to join and seek the protection of an existing local party. The Tarar brothers inherited land as *nanki virsa* in the village of Mohla. Their father's property was in Mitha Chak, a village eighteen miles away, and as it was smaller than the *nanki virsa,* four of the brothers came to settle in Mohla while the fifth remained in their native village to manage the property there. After some time, one of the brothers had a love affair with his mother's sister's daughter, who lived in the neighboring village. The girl became pregnant, and her *biraderis* were very angry and wanted to beat up the four brothers. One of the Tarar brothers came to the *chowdhri* of Mohla and begged for help for "they had no *biraderi* in Mohla to support them." The *chowdhri* promised his protection, and no one dared to attack them. Now the four men are quite well assimilated in the village, but whenever they try to intrigue or to form a party, they are immediately reminded that they do not belong to Mohla.

After having lived in Mohla for twenty years, they hurt the feelings of the local *kammis* by doing them an injustice on the occasion of the marriage of their sister. According to custom, when the bride leaves for the home of her parents-in-law for the first time, she is accompanied by the wife of the village barber, who in this capacity is called a *dayin* and is entitled to receive a substantial gift from the parents-in-law of the bride—a buffalo or golden ornaments worth 125–150 rupees. But instead of asking the barber's wife in Mohla, who had been their *seypi* for years and was looking forward to the occasion to receive the gift, the Tarar brothers brought in a *mirasin*, the wife of the village bard, from their original village. The *mirasin* accompanied the bride and received the present, and everyone in the village felt indignant. Besides, the brothers called the *kammis* from their native village to help at the marriage ceremonies and distributed *laag*, the money given to *kammis* on big occasions, among them. By so doing, they disregarded the rights of the *kammis* who had become their *seypis* in Mohla as well as of all the other *kammis* who belonged in this village.

This situation proved again how little an outsider cares for the people, the relationships, and the collective unity basic to village organization.

V

The Farmer's Calendar

Land cultivation is a year-round occupation. The farmer has times of intense work followed by relatively slack seasons.[1] His two busiest periods are the seasons of summer and autumn harvesting and planting.

For the farmer the sun and the rain are the two main factors in connection with agriculture. The scorching heat of the summer sun and the time of year when the rain starts, its intensity, and duration are of greatest importance to him. Midsummer is the usual time for the monsoon rains. Before the rains come, to have a blazing sun, when even birds look for a shady nook, is a blessing to the farmer, who works all day long to get through the most intensive work of the year, the harvesting of the main crops—wheat, barley, and gram —which he had planted the previous fall.

The much awaited monsoon brings hope on the one hand and despair on the other. The farmer is full of hope, for the rains mean enough water to start the planting of the paddy, but if the rains last too long this means flood, and flood is destructive. It may demolish his house, destroy his fields, leave the standing sugarcane and fodder covered with mud, and carry away the straw stored for the cattle.

Nevertheless, with the first shower he is busy planting the paddy. After that, until the early fall, he has little to do except for the

---

[1] See also Appendix II, The Farmer's Round of Activities, for an outline of the apportionment of time in the farming year.

routine work of caring for his cattle, cutting and preparing fodder for them, weeding the paddy fields, and, if there is a long interval between the rains, irrigating the fields. Thus between his hopes and fears, the time goes on, and if the monsoon rains do not cause devastation he has his autumn crop of paddy and also millet and maize.

The autumn harvest, *kharif,* also known as *sauni,* starts in the

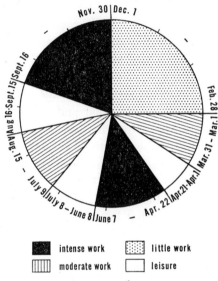

FIGURE 1. FARMER'S CALENDAR

middle of September and continues through November. This is a very busy season, for the farmer has both to harvest the crops in the different fields as they ripen and to prepare for sowing the fallow fields that have been lying under water during the rainy season and are now drying out. If the soil has retained the dampness of the rains, it is easier for him to plough, but if it has not rained, the soil is dry and he has to irrigate these fields, which is extra work and takes much time. It takes at least sixteen hours to irrigate each field. With a plough drawn by a pair of oxen, it takes him one day to plough one field thoroughly, and he has to plough each field at least four or five times. In these fields he sows the main crops of the year—wheat, barley, and gram. At the same time he also plants the winter vegetables—carrots, turnips, radishes, cauliflower, and lentils. Also in the late fall the paddy is ripe and he must harvest it. So this is a period of intense activity, when the farmer may need all of the twenty-four hours of a day for work. If he can get it, he asks for help.

This season of intensive work is followed by a period of relative rest, the three winter months, when, if it rains, as it usually does, the crop sown in the fall will grow abundantly, producing plenty of fodder for the cattle. However, if it does not rain, the farmer must irrigate the wheat and other crops, the vegetables, and also the fields which are to be ploughed and prepared for the early spring sowing. If it were not for the lack of fodder, this would be an easy period for him. If he has stored enough wheat, barley, and gram, he grinds them coarsely and mixes them with hay to feed his animals. They are then well fed. But usually he does not have enough; then he cuts off the tops of sugarcane and collects grass, if there are lowlands nearby, but he still has a hard time keeping his animals fed.

In the early spring he plants sugarcane, tobacco, fodder, chili peppers, melons, and summer vegetables in the fields he ploughed during the winter months.

In the late spring he is free, but he is under great pressure of food shortage in this "thirteenth month," as he calls it. It is the period when the supply of wheat and other grains is exhausted, the new crop is still in the fields, and he has to manage by borrowing— but no one has enough to lend anyone else. Though it is a brief period, it is a difficult one and seems very long.

Then in the summer, the wheat, barley, and gram are again ready to be harvested. This is the summer harvest, *rabi*, commonly known as *haṛi*, the busiest period of the year for everyone. The crop must be cut, threshed, and winnowed, and all the people who have been working for the farmer during the past year must be paid in grain. The grain for the year must be stored away, as also the straw for the animals. During this busy period of harvest, he has also to irrigate the fields of tobacco, chilies, sugarcane, fodder, and summer vegetables, which he planted in the early spring, for now the days are hot and dry. He also plants a nursery for the paddy, cotton, and the fodder which he always needs for his cattle.

After he has stored the wheat and has collected the tobacco, the farmer has plenty and for one month there is not much to do, except for the routine work of weeding, turning the soil, irrigating, and taking care of the cattle.

This is the month of country fairs which the farmer attends, where he listens to music and singing, watches wrestling, horse races, and native games, eats sweets and fruits, and enjoys life thoroughly.

Then the cycle of work begins anew.

While the work of the farmer is to cultivate the land and to take care of the cattle, the work of the farmer's wife—besides her regular tasks of cooking, washing, and house cleaning—is to store, preserve, and make ready for consumption the produce of the land and of the cattle.

She molds large clay bins for storing the yearly supply of wheat and plasters them inside and out before the new crop is to come in. After the rainy season, she plasters the roof, on which wheat is spread to dry, for during the rains everything becomes moldy. If there are worms in the grain, her husband will winnow the grain before it is stored again. From this wheat she brings out as much as is needed for a week, cleans and grinds it as she finds time. Some of it she grinds several times; she keeps this very fine flour for making sweets or vermicelli.

While the paddy is not yet fully ripe, the farmer brings some of it home, where the wife threshes and roasts it and mixes it with sugar and sesame seeds to be chewed in the afternoons by young girls and women. She sends some to her married daughter and to relatives who live in localities where rice is not grown, and gives some to friends and neighbors whose paddy is not ready yet and also to the wives of the craftsmen who work for her family. This mixture of rice, sugar, and sesame seeds is a delicacy and a special treat for it cannot be bought.

Then in the fall the cotton is ready. If cotton is grown as a cash crop, there will be several women to pick it and they are paid in kind; but if there is only one field, then the farmer's wife takes with her the wife of a craftsman for whom it is a favor to be allowed to help pick the cotton for she will get some also.

Once the cotton is brought home, the farmer's wife dries it, grades it for quality, beats it with a stick until the dried leaves and dust sticking to it pass through the holes of the cot on which it has been placed, and passes it through a small wooden ginning machine to remove the seeds, which are used to feed the cattle. She then gives it to the weaver who fluffs it out, after which she makes small rolls, which she will spin during the long winter evenings when a few women friends will come together to chat and spin. Some of the thread she spins is coarse and some very fine, depending on how it will be used—whether for native blankets, cloth for ordinary use, or cloth for men's shirts. She then takes the skeins to the weaver, who starches the thread to serve as the warp and weaves it for her.

When the chilies ripen in the fields, she collects them and makes pickles. Pickles are an important item in the diet throughout the year; besides the green chilies she also pickles lemons, green mangoes, and sometimes horseradish. Some of the chilies are left in the field to be picked after they have turned red; these are dried and stored to be used in nearly every dish.

When the maize is ripe, she breaks it from the stalks, and at home husks it and dries it; then some evening she calls some strong adolescent boys, who beat the corn with clubs to separate the grain from the cob. They get some corn for this work. Then she grinds the corn and makes corn bread. Some of the corn is left on the cob to be dried and put away to make popcorn, which women and children chew between meals. Some of the unhusked cobs she sends to her relatives in other villages where corn is not grown, and some she also gives to her friends and neighbors and to the wives of the craftsmen who work for the household. In making a distribution, people see to it that every family in the village, rich or poor, get a share, no matter how little, of each new crop and fruit as it is brought home.

When the bulk of the paddy crop is brought home, the farmer's wife dries it and sends it to be husked at the mill, which begins to work in winter. After it comes back from the mill, she separates the whole grains of rice from the broken ones by passing them through a sieve. The whole grain is roasted and stored, for the best rice is at least two years old and is used on special occasions. The rest of the rice is for daily use.

Fresh sugarcane is brought home to be sucked by men, women, and children. But the larger part of the sugarcane is crushed, boiled, and made into brown sugar; this work is done by the men in a special place in the fields. Brown sugar is used throughout the year in food and in tea, fed to the cattle, and also distributed on special occasions.

During the harvest season, the farmer's wife goes gleaning. She also plasters the threshing ground in the fields. During the year she raises chickens and, whenever she can spare them, sells the eggs to a hawker who goes through the villages.

VI

The Village in Winter

Unlike the months from spring through autumn, when hardly a man is to be seen in the village, for all are working in the fields, winter is the season when the throb of life is felt outside the mud walls of the compounds, especially on the side of the village which faces south and gets the most sun. Winter days are warm and sunny; as it is much warmer outside than inside the houses, people spend the day outdoors.

Men go out into the morning sun and warm themselves until they feel ready to go to work, their main concern during this slack agricultural season being to provide fodder for the cattle. They choose sunny spots and sit in small groups smoking the *huka,* each man passing it on to the next after he has inhaled no more than three times. Some are lounging on the ground and some on the cots crowded in a sunny place. One of them is reciting verses of a popular Punjabi poem which they all know and never tire of hearing. Landowners and craftsmen, *zamindars* and *kammis,* sit in the same group; a *zamindar* may sit or lie on a cot while a *kammi* perches on its edge or squats on the ground or on the low wall of the compound surrounding the men's guest house.

Most of the craftsmen worked in the fields during the busy agricultural season and helped the farmer in ploughing, irrigating, and harvesting, for then agricultural work is the main source of income. But now they can devote their time to their crafts which bring them additional income.

The cobbler is working in his workshop, which is in one corner of his house. The tailor sits cross legged in front of his sewing machine on the veranda of his house. His wife helps him; both are kept very busy, for very few of the village women ever use a needle. One weaver stretches cotton yarn across an unploughed field, and his wife and daughter help him to starch it. The other weavers work in a special place protected by a roof and a wall on one side, each sitting in a pit in front of his handloom, weaving cotton blankets or coarse cloth. A *musalli,* agricultural laborer, weaves straw mats on the porch of a house which looks like a city house; he is the caretaker of this place whose owners live in the city but still maintain a house in the village where they have relatives and own land.

The potter made the bulk of his earthenware utensils and delivered them to his clients well before the harvest. During the harvest he helped with the transport of grain to the market and to the houses. Now he transports clay and sand and the sun-dried bricks used in construction. He also collects dung from his clients and stores it for use in his kiln.

The baker is also busy, for winter is the fishing season. By occupation, the baker is a hunter of small game and a fisherman, although those who live far away from the rivers and large ponds do not practice this occupation. During the summer the baker collected and stored enough fuel to heat the oven in which his wife bakes bread. Now the few bakers of the village, all of whom are relatives, *biraderis,* are settled near the bank of the river, which is a short distance away, and come home only occasionally. They sell their catch of fish at the city market, but two or three times during the fishing season they bring fish to the village to give to their clients who have their bread baked in their ovens. This gift is made in the same spirit as is shown by the landowner when he sends a little of the first crop of fruit, grain, or vegetables to his friends and to the craftsmen who work for his family. And the baker's wife who brings a gift of fish to her clients is not sent away empty handed, but is given some grain. Bakers do not usually sell fish in their village, for they have a contract with a fish dealer in the city, but if people request them to bring some fish, which is regarded as a strengthening food and as one good for curing colds, they will do so.

The *musalliñ*, the wife of an agricultural laborer, also is busy in the village, going with her large broom to the houses of the land-owners for whom she works. There she sweeps the courtyard where the sucked sugarcane, the vegetable peels, the corn cobs, and every other kind of refuse have been carelessly thrown on the ground throughout the day. She also collects the dung at the place where the buffaloes were tied, shapes them into round cakes, and sticks them on the outside wall, where they look like a magnified honey-comb. Little girls, too, collect dung in the streets and shape it into dung cakes, which they take home to be used as fuel.

While the craftsmen follow their professions, providing for the cattle, especially in the winter months when fodder is short, is a task of primary importance to everyone, landowner and craftsman. In winter, the cattle remain in the village. Although most people have separate rooms for cattle in their courtyards or, if they do not, keep them in someone else's cattle stall, in the daytime the cattle are tied in the sunshine. Men and boys over ten go to the fields to weed and return carrying on their heads loads of fodder so huge that they can scarcely be seen under them. Once a day the cattle are taken to the pond to drink and to wade.

Cattle are of the utmost importance to this agricultural people. A farmer needs cattle for the plough and at the well. Cattle drop-pings are used as fertilizer, and the *kammis* also use them as fuel. Besides, cattle are a source of food and of income for all the village people, *zamindars* and *kammis* alike. A family which has a buffalo is provided for. Although there are a few cows, people prefer to have a buffalo. Cattle give them milk, from which they get butter-milk and butter, some of which is clarified to make *ghi*. Some of the *ghi* is used by the families themselves, but the women try to save some for sale. Sometimes people buy *ghi* from a neighbor in the village. Then there is a man who goes through the villages collecting *ghi* to sell in the cities, so usually women are well informed about its current price. With the money from its sale, women buy salt, sugar, kerosene, soap, and other grocery items. Men care for the cattle and milk them, but women have sole charge of the milk and its products.

People take good care of their cattle and feed them before they eat their own meal. When a buffalo calves, the family rejoices greatly, for in three years the young buffalo will be worth a considerable sum of money. When a visitor comes, he inquires after the health of the family and also asks if the host's buffalo is giving milk, for a wet buffalo means that the family is at ease. The death of a buffalo is deeply mourned. On such occasions neighbors and friends and people from the neighboring villages come to offer condolences. To sympathize in sorrow is part of the exchange relationship existing between the villages.

By the time the sun is quite high, the woman at home has finished her morning chores. She rose before sunrise and in the dim light of a small lamp started to grind the grain. The sound of the grinding mill reaches the children in their beds, but they sleep on. Then she begins to churn the milk; in spring and summer she would churn outside, but now this is done in the room. The children wake up, but still remain for some time in bed, while the mother lets the chickens out from under the large basket with which they were covered at night. Then she kneads the dough and lights the fire. The children come outside and warm themselves near the hearth. They do not change their clothes for they sleep in the same clothes they wear during the day. They eat bread with butter and pickles, drink buttermilk, and go to the mosque.

Not every woman cooks on winter mornings. Some give the children bread or rice from the previous evening with buttermilk. In some houses people eat both breakfast and lunch, but other women prefer to prepare an early lunch.

Children hardly wash their hands and faces in the mornings, for they are cold and the mother doesn't insist too much. She will wash them in the afternoon when it gets warm, and will change their clothes. The woman herself changes into fresh clothes in the afternoon, after she has finished her work, has washed, and has combed her hair; she finds little time in the morning to attend to her toilette.

Men do not wash themselves at home. They go either to the well or to the bath attached to the mosque. A man wraps himself in an old sheet and sits in the sun while his wife washes and dries his clothes.

After the children leave, the woman washes the dishes from the previous evening and from the morning, and feeds the chickens. She rolls up the bedding and puts it away, and carries the cots out into the courtyard for they are used during the day. A neighbor may stop in for a few minutes, but morning is a busy time.

The smoke rising over the walls of the baker's house is a sign that the oven is being heated. The baker's wife heats the oven twice before noon on winter mornings—for the people who eat an early lunch and for those who eat after noon. The baker's wife, as she works, squats by the side of an earthenware oven sunk in the ground. A small roof protects her from too much sunshine. Other women squat around her with their earthenware platters of dough which they shape into flat round breads and pass to the baker's wife to stick to the sides of the heated oven. For every eight loaves baked, she lays aside a piece of dough for one loaf as payment for her work. But even though she is paid every time bread is baked, at harvest time the *zamindars* who are her customers send her some grain. While they wait for their bread to be baked, women's tongues are as busy as their hands. This is the social club for women, where they exchange all the news and gossip of the village: how many outfits a certain woman brought from her visit to her parents' home; how, to spite her daughter-in-law, a farmer's mother was trying to persuade her son to take a second wife; and how the weavers threatened to leave the village unless the daughter of a weaver who had eloped with the son of a poor *zamindar* was returned to her parents.

The bread baked, the woman goes home and places an earthenware pot with lentils on the fire, or sometimes she will crush radishes or mint with salt and red chilies to be eaten with bread. In the evenings she may cook some vegetables, carrots or turnips which she or her children may have picked in the fields. During the day there will usually come women vendors of the *araiñ*, the vegetable growers' caste, who bring vegetables from the neighboring village.

As the sun rises higher and if the well is working, some women go there with their laundry, which they have soaked in boiling water and washing soda, and, placing a washboard under the running water, they beat the clothes with a wooden club, rub them with soap, and rinse them out. They spread the clothes to dry on the grass in the fields next to the well. The dry clothes are not ironed. While the clothes are drying, a woman squats and washes herself in a small enclosure through which a thick jet of water from the well runs on its way to the fields. When the well is working, it is always a busy place.

While the little children are playing by the well, the older boys are in the mosque, where they go for an hour every day to learn to read the Koran from the village *imam*, and the girls study in the *imam's* house under the tutoring of his wife. This is the extent of the children's formal education. There are thirty chapters in the Koran containing altogether one hundred and fourteen *suras*, or sections, and most of the boys will not get beyond the third chapter. Instead, they help their fathers in their work and thus, if their fathers are *kammis*, learn their fathers' trade. All boys learn how to cultivate the land and take care of the cattle. The girls are more ambitious in their studies. Some may finish reading the Koran, an occasion on which the *imam* and his wife will get new outfits, a tray of food, and, if the girl's parents are well off, even a young buffalo. Otherwise, for his teaching, the parents send the *imam* a bushel of grain at each harvest.

Boys and girls play together. Little girls, carrying their baby siblings on their hips, join the other children in their play, and all treat the babies with great affection. Whenever there is a gathering, children are there. If they make noise while the men are gathered to discuss a matter of importance, someone may warn them, but never strictly. Yet the children are taught to speak and behave with respect toward any older person, whatever his status.

Children come home in time for lunch. They know by looking at the sun when the time comes and do not need to be called.

The village *imam* comes in to collect his bread, for every house gives him one bread and he gets two at the house of the *chowdhri,* where he also gets a tray of food on Thursday evenings.

The afternoon is the time for leisure and for visiting. A few women neighbors may drop in, and they all sit crowded together on a cot. Someone may read the popular poem, for women love it, too. The barber's wife or his mother may drop in, but she does not stay very long for she is on her way to the *chowdhri's* house where she will wash and comb and braid the *chowdhrani's* hair and will also massage her body, for this is her duty.

The children come running in from the street, for the vendor of bangles has come. The man stays in the lane and sends in the bangles and tells the price. Women and girls love to wear glass bangles. The wife and the sister of the *chowdhri* have gold bracelets, but just the same the colorful bangles appeal to them as well. The bangles, which should fit snugly just above the wrist, are tried on and even baby girls get a set of them for each arm.

Women also love earrings, and some have nose plugs. Only old women do not wear ornaments, except for the old *chowdhrani,* who wears a gold ring. Little girls are given silver or gold earrings when they are about five. Old women have a number of holes around the edge of each ear, but that is a past fashion; the younger ones have only one hole in each lobe. The ear plug is seldom worn and although some of the young women have had their nose pierced, they do not wear a nose plug. No little girl, with the exception of the *imam's* daughter, has her nose pierced nowadays. In this district people follow closely the fashion that emanates from Lahore and reaches the small towns nearby.

The women know the latest design in yard goods as well. A vendor of cloth passes twice a week through the village, and the women examine the cloth he carries, inquire about prices, and may buy material for a shirt or a headscarf or a *tahmud*, a cloth draped around the waist that hangs down to the ankles. It is not easy to buy material for a whole outfit, and the three piece costume is seldom replaced at once. So the bright color of the headscarf stands out against the faded cloth beneath it. However, women like to dye their clothes, especially their headscarves, to match the rest of their costumes, and the village shop is never short of dyes. Once in ten days the *zamindar* woman herself goes to the city. She may go with the barber's mother or with some wives of *kammis*. There she buys groceries, cottonseed for the buffalo, and goes through the cloth shops.

There are always people from the outside who pass through the village. There are the vendors who sell children's toys, cheap crockery, and fruit; the men who pewter the copper pots; in summer, the ice cream man; a juggler; a man with a trained monkey and a bear; a group of professionals whose specialty it is to sing a lullaby to a baby; a village bard who travels with an orphaned son; a traveling fakir; a beggar—all stop on their way to the villages beyond. The fakir knocks on the door and announces that he is a fakir; the beggar begs in the name of God. They usually know which are the doors to knock at, and people give them grain or food—never leftovers, for that is a sin.

The children run home in midafternoon to get some grain to have roasted at the baker's. The little girls tie a handful in the corner of their headscarves; the little boys put it in the side pocket of their shirts. The mother at the same time offers some in a copper plate placed in front of her visitors.

In the men's guest house, a small group of men play cards—a cobbler, the driver of a carriage who has come back from the city early in the afternoon, a *zamindar,* and the old servant of the *chowdhri.* A few men are also watching them. They play bridge and trumpet card, and are intent on playing their best, for they never play for money but are proud to play well.

Late in the afternoon some men come in from the fields laden with huge piles of fodder. Others go home to milk the buffaloes. The children are already at home, playing in the courtyard.

As sunset nears, a few men go to the mosque to take their ablutions. Women who pray take their ablutions at home. Sunset is announced by the chanting of the call to prayer from the veranda of the mosque. Silence falls on the men sitting outside, as each says a prayer in his heart. Women pray on small mats spread in the courtyards or on the verandas of their homes. When the prayer is over, the men go home for their evening meal. But on their way they stop and gaze toward the west, where in the darkening sky they can discern the silver thread of the crescent moon. Everyone waits for the new moon, and after saying a prayer while looking at the moon they disperse.

The evening meal is served right after sunset. The family squat near the hearth, except for the father who sits on a cot and is served there. After the meal, men get together in small groups. If they have work or some intrigue to discuss, they will visit each other's houses; otherwise they leave their houses and go outside to the places they usually frequent—the men's guest house, the place where some wealthy landowner keeps his cattle, or the workshop of the cobbler who always keeps a fresh *huka.* Young men and boys join the older men or sit and tell stories or guess at riddles.

Women also visit in the evenings. Young and old sit together. Young girls vie with one another in spinning. Girls and small boys stay with the women and soon fall asleep. The women move the cots. Children up to ten sleep with mothers, aunts, and grandmothers.

In the life of the village people, which is close to nature, the moon is not only a source of light but also means safety and joy. The new moon brings new hope and gladness and serenity to the people; seeing it, they give the glad tidings to one another, "The new moon!"

During the dark of the moon, people are afraid of thefts, for the great majority of thefts occur in the few nights preceding the appearance of the new moon. Then as the people watch the new moon they feel safer, and toward the fifteenth of the moon, when the village is bathed in its light, a man can leave his house open as he would in the daytime.

A farmer working at the well or a fisherman going to the river much prefers a moonlit night. Men and women like to visit on such nights. Young men and adolescent boys roam in the fields and sing and frolic. When someone from another village is asked to visit, he says he will come on a moonlit night.

Everything becomes quiet after the night prayer. The only sound heard is the tinkling of the bells of the buffaloes working at the well, the regular flow of the water, and the song of a young man who is working at the well the whole night.

VII

The Calendar of Religion

While agricultural activities follow the seasons and are closely related to the cycle of rain and sun, religious activities are closely related to the moon. With regard to the time for ploughing, sowing, and harvesting the different crops, people know and use the Punjabi months, a farmer's calendar, but when it comes to the practice of their religion, they use the lunar months of the Muslim calendar.[1]

However, most people know the names only of those of the lunar months which mark special religious holidays. People always watch the waxing and the waning of the moon, and women count the days of the moon, for the eleventh day of each moon is the day for charity. Then, in homes that are better off, rice, bread, and some meat dish are prepared in abundance and distributed among the people. Women and children know well which house has cooked food for distribution and are ready with their bowls to receive it. The children of both *kammis* and poor *zamindars* come to get this food, but among women, only the wives of *kammis* would come.

On the twelfth day of Rabi-ul-Avval, which is the third month of the Muslim calendar, people celebrate the birth of the Prophet, the Id Milad, the festival of nativity. On that day well-to-do *zamindars*

---

[1] Because the Punjabi months are those of the Gregorian calendar while the Muslim calendar is one of 29 or 30 days, according to the appearance of the new moon, there is no fixed relationship between secular and religious activities, whose occurrence changes annually.

and *kammis* cook rice, the *imam* says a prayer over it, and then it is distributed in the village.

Each month brings people closer to the holy month of Ramzan, of fasting, which is the ninth month of the Muslim calendar. By praying, fasting, and abstaining from all indulgences, by being kind and just, people feel that they may share in the blessings of God which abound during this month of Ramzan.

Two weeks before the fast begins, people celebrate the night of Shab-e-barat, which they believe is the time when the destinies of people are fixed for the year ahead and when the names of those who are to die during the year are taken off the list up above. People cook special food and give food to the poor in the village and to beggars, and those who have quarreled make up.

During the month of Ramzan, men and women fast, that is, they do not eat or drink or smoke during the day until sunset. After the evening meal they eat once more before sunrise. They watch the stars and know when it is time to eat. Then the baker heats the oven and knocks on the doors of his clients and tells them to bring the dough to be baked in his oven. During the day people go about their work as usual, but they pray more and most men assemble for the evening prayer at the mosque, where at sunset they break their fast by eating one date or drinking a glass of milk or a sweetened drink, such as lemonade. Throughout the month, the houses of well-to-do *kammis* and *zamindars* send to the mosque pitchers of soft, sweetened drinks or fruit for the men when they break their fast. After the evening prayer is said, people go home for their meal. Toward the end of Ramzan, the sky is scanned eagerly for the new moon which heralds the day of Id, the holiday. Even though it is cloudy, there is always someone who brings the news from the city that the next day is the Id.

Early in the morning of this day, women cook sweet vermicelli, which they have been preparing during the preceding month. Everybody wears festive clothes. All the men and the adolescent boys go to the mosque to pray. Swings are tied from the trees for the children. Young girls come in groups to the house of the *chowdhri* and to the houses of their friends and beat on empty pitchers and sing songs. Following the regular practice in Islam, every house, except for the poorest, gives away grain to the poor and the crippled; the amount given is in accordance with the number of people in the donor's household, including the servants. The *kammis* come to greet the *zamindars* and receive freshly cooked food and newly baked bread and money. A tray of food is sent to a married daughter if she is in a nearby village.

It is the women who are in charge of the distribution, for it is they who know what and how much should be given and to whom. They cook, or have the barber cook, the food which they themselves distribute to those who come to the house; to those who may not be able to come, they send a plate of food by the barber's wife.

People also know the month of Haj, when pilgrimage is made to Mecca, for to make that pilgrimage is the most cherished wish of men and women. There may even be someone from the village who will go on the pilgrimage. Before the person, man or woman, departs, all the relatives are called to come and stay for a few days. The relatives bring clothes or money for the person who is leaving, and the family cooks and distributes food in great quantities in the village, as well as giving gifts of clothes to the daughters, the nieces, and the granddaughters, and gifts of money to the *kammis* and the poor.

On the Id-ul-Bakr, the day following the Haj or the tenth day of the month of Haj, in accordance with the practice of Islam, people celebrate the holiday by sacrificing a sheep, or several families join together and sacrifice a cow. The meat of the sacrificed animal is cut into small pieces which are mixed up so the whole is of uniform quality. This meat is divided into three equal parts. One part is for the kin, one for the household, and one for non-kin, actually the poor. The portion for the kin is placed on plates corresponding in number to the number of households of relatives in the village, and these are sent to their homes. The portion for the non-kin is distributed among the people who come to the house to ask for it; these may be *kammi* women, the wives and children of poor *zamindars,* or beggars. Sometimes meat is sent to those who are poor but are unable to come. The portion set aside for the house may not be entirely used by the household, because as the poor come they are not turned away but are given from that portion of meat also. To sacrifice an animal is obligatory for those who can afford it; but sometimes a poor man may have a desire to sacrifice an animal and will do so. On one such holiday in Mohla, three cows and five sheep were sacrificed. All the people of the village had meat to eat. People see to it that no one is left out.

And then people know the first month of the Muslim calendar, Muharram, the month of mourning. At this time men and young boys repair the graves. People send for fresh flowers, say a prayer over them, and strew petals of roses, jasmin, and marigold over the graves.

On the tenth day of Muharram, well-to-do *zamindars* and *kammis* cook plenty of rice and sweet syrup for distribution. Everybody in the village knows which houses have cooked food for the occasion. The wives of poor *kammis* of the village go there and are given rice and syrup in small cups and saucers which have been made to order by the potter. Children of the rich and poor alike flock to those houses and are given rice and syrup. The custom is never to refuse food to children.

The month of Muharram is followed by the month of Safar, which according to local belief is a month of great hardships in the history of Islam. Much charity is given during this month, and when the beggars appear at the door people give them larger amounts of grain than they would at other times of the year. A rich *zamindar* may give two to four pounds of wheat. (In the course of one year, the house of the *chowdhri* of Mohla gave about 400 pounds of grain to beggars.) Beggars are also given clothes.

The seventh month of the Muslim calendar is Rajjab. Some people do not know it by name, but they know that this is the month of giving *zakat,* the annual assessment imposed by Islam on one's excess property. No one is forced to give; a person's own conscience compels him to give. People assess their property—houses, with the exception of the house they live in, livestock, golden ornaments, money in the bank or hoarded money, profits made in business—and compute 2.5 percent of its total value and give this money to the poor and the sick, widows and orphans. This is *zakat.* People believe that by giving *zakat* their property becomes *pak,* purified and blessed, and will always be under the protection of God. They also believe that a man who is honest in giving his *zakat* will be blessed in any enterprise and will profit from it.

The other months of the lunar calendar do not stand out clearly in people's minds, for they are not important to them. Besides celebrating the holidays, at different times of the year people go to attend *urs*—the anniversary of the death of some *pir,* religious leader, held at his tomb. The celebrations are organized by the descendants of the *pir* or by his disciples who for this occasion cook great quantities of food. All the followers of the *pir* come together. They bring gifts of money, *ghi,* grain, and cotton blankets, which go to the caretaker of the place.

People pray, fast, celebrate religious holidays, welcome the new moon, do charity, know about the fundamental tenets of Islam, and some can and do read the Koran—that is part of their daily life. Their attitude is that God is with them, not to punish but to help. At a time of flood, when the soaked walls of their houses tumble down in a heap and the cattle are carried away in a muddy torrent, they help one another to collect what is left of their possessions and, the moment the waters withdraw, start to build their houses again. There is no feeling of despair or of challenge. God is never against them, "He knows best." People will look wistfully at their wasted fields after a swarm of locusts has devoured the standing crop and say, "It's the will of Allah." At a time of death, they mourn but never feel that the death was a punishment from above, for "Allah knows what is best for them."

Many women in the village pray regularly five times a day and fast during the whole month of Ramzan. Some women seldom pray, but most of them fast. A few men pray regularly, even when they are in the fields; when they are in the village they go to the mosque. The rest keep hushed silence whenever *azan* is chanted. On Fridays more men attend the village mosque, and some go to the city to pray. On Id all the men and all the boys in the village go to the mosque for the morning prayer. People know the fundamentals of their religion, which are so interwoven with their lives that they are a way of life to them.

However, people try to go beyond the practices of formalized religion in their understanding. They seek for the real meaning in prayer, fasting, and other religious practices. Many question the purpose of man's existence. They feel that man has been created for some higher purpose, but that his striving to satisfy his earthly needs has forced him away from the *suratum mustakim*—the straight path. Consciousness of not being on the straight path makes people wonder and question themselves. Most men and women at some time in their lives, after they have struggled within themselves, come to the point at which they feel the need for spiritual guidance. The village *imam* serves only the needs of the formalized rituals of religion. People feel that in order to discipline themselves so as to reach God they need the help of someone who is on the straight path, and for this guidance they turn to the *pirs*, the spiritual leaders.

People strive to reach God through prayer and contemplation and by reciting poetry—the popular romantic poems *Hir Ranja* and *Saif-ul-Mulk*, in which the love of man and woman is symbolic of the love of God. Each one has to reach God through his own efforts, for that experience can neither be explained nor taught but should be achieved by the seeker himself.

The path to reach God is open to all, rich or poor, man or woman. A poor cobbler—as happened in Mohla—who is further ahead on this straight path than a rich *zamindar* has the respect of everybody. This spiritual struggle is the essence of the religious life of the people and it unites those who seek and those who have the desire to seek but have not yet reached the point at which they feel ready for spiritual guidance.

At least once a year people invite to the village a *pir* under whose guidance they seek "to attain" their way. Some families have their own *pir*, on whom they call whenever they feel the need, to whom they make contributions, and whom they sometimes invite to a big meal, feeling honored by his presence. This would be the *pir* who has the largest following in the village and the vicinity.

Before the coming of the *pir*, young boys and men whitewash the mosque, clean the vacant plot in front, draw white lines on the ground leading to the mosque, and plant green branches beside them, forming an *allée*. Colored paper streamers fly from strings stretched across the compound of the mosque. A big armchair and a table are placed for the *pir* on the veranda of the mosque. The neighboring villages are notified of the date of the coming of the *pir*.

In the late afternoon of the day, the *pir* and his retinue are met by a group of men on the outskirts of the village and are royally entertained at the house of one of the *pir's* followers. Sometimes it is the *chowdhri's* family who sends the food. Later, fruit, raisins, and small pieces of sweets from the *pir's* table are given to as many people as possible in the village, for this food is *tabaruk*, that is, it carries blessings with it.

In the courtyard, where mats are spread for them, and outside the walls of the mosque, the men crowd; among them are men from the neighboring villages. Women and children sit crowded together on the roofs of the houses overlooking the mosque. One of the men who came with the *pir* beautifully chants religious songs in which are described the life and death of the Prophet. Then the *pir* explains to the people the meaning of various aspects of religion. He usually speaks forcefully and effectively so that the people are deeply stirred. Some of the men in the mosque sob; the women weep. The sermon and the chanting last well into the night. The children, feeling miserable, fall asleep on the cots outside, but their mothers are too much moved to attend to them.

On the following morning breakfast is prepared for the *pir* by a family other than the one which entertained him in the evening, for it is a great privilege to do so. After breakfast, people call on the *pir* and bring him presents of money, grain, or cotton blankets. Then the *pir* and his followers leave the village.

VIII

The Family and the Kin Group

The primary social unit in Punjabi society is that group of people who live together in one household. A man speaks of his immediate family as *mera ghar,* which means "my house."

This household unit may include only the members of the conjugal family of husband, wife, and children, if a married man lives apart from his parents and siblings. Or it may include all the members of a joint family, that is, the aged father and mother, married sons with their wives and children, unmarried sons and daughters, and occasionally a widowed daughter with or without her children. Or, after the sons and daughters are grown up and have been established in marriage, the household may take the form of a stem family, including the aged parents and one of the sons—usually the youngest—with his wife and children. After the parents' death, this son remains in the paternal home. Another type of joint family, consisting of a group of brothers living in one compound, is also common. If a younger son has not yet married at the time of his parents' death, he will live with one of his married brothers who arranges his marriage. A joint household consisting of a group of brothers may separate if their wives do not get along. But the brothers may keep their property intact and continue to work together, because brothers usually get along well, but in the compound they may have separate cooking arrangements. As their children grow up, they usually establish separate compounds but still go on having property in common.

As will be discussed in the following chapter, the group living together in one compound may be regarded as consisting of one or of several distinct households, depending upon whether the adult married sons and their wives have taken upon themselves responsibility for carrying on certain activities with kin and non-kin— primarily those concerned with institutionalized gift exchange, *vartan bhanji*. Each of the several households in one compound may be referred to as a "hearth."

Thus it is clear that coresidence in a compound may have different implications under a variety of circumstances, and that the unit which comprises a household is a very flexible one, which may or may not coincide with the total group resident in a compound.

Sometimes the word *ṭabr* is also used to refer to the household unit; besides meaning the conjugal or the joint family, it can also be used to refer to the members of the patrilineage. However, a clear distinction is made between members of the kin group who are more nearly and those who are more distantly related. Father and son, brother and sister are called *apna*, one's own; uncles, cousins, and other more distant relatives in the male line of descent are the *biraderi*.

The line of demarcation between one's own family and the *biraderi* as well as the essential unity of the two are expressed in a proverb: "One does not share the bread but one shares the blame." That is, a family owns property in common and consequently shares income and expenditures, but the *biraderis*, who live in different households, each with its own shared income, are affected by the wrongdoing of any one of its members in whatever household he belongs and their prestige suffers thereby.

BIRADERI

A *biraderi* is a patrilineage. All the men who can trace their relationship to a common ancestor, no matter how remote, belong to the same *biraderi*. The term *kabila* (an Arabic word) is also used, but *biraderi* is the term in more common use. *Biraderi* refers both to the whole group of those who belong to a patrilineage and to any individual member of a patrilineage. Daughters belong to the *biraderi* of their fathers, but after marriage are included in the *biraderi* of their husbands also. All the members of a *biraderi* are considered to be relatives, with the exception of those whose exact links to the other members cannot be established. Such persons are said to be *biraderi,* but they are not accepted as kin.

Some of the *biraderis* in the village are known collectively by the name of their common ancestor. This is more typical of, though not limited to, the *biraderis* of *kammis,* whose members recognize as a common ancestor a person not more than two generations removed. In Mohla, such is the *biraderi* of the weavers, who are known as *Davlu-da,* meaning those who belong to the *biraderi* of Davlu, their common ancestor. However, in a neighboring village there are two *biraderis* of *zamindars* known as *Vassu-ka* and *Mehr-ka,* whose common ancestors are, respectively, Vassu and Mehr. Other *zamindar biraderis* are called after their subcaste. For example, there were the *biraderis* of Cheema, Vṛech, Chattha, Gondl, and so on. The name Cheema or Vṛech may go back to some far off common ancestor after whom the subcaste became known.

The term *biraderi* may also be used in an extended sense, when it refers to a group of people who are not kin. Thus in its extended meaning, *biraderi* may refer to all the *zamindars* who live in one village, or in a locality, or throughout the country. Among the *kammis,* the barbers who live in one village or all those throughout the country are *biraderi,* as are also all the bakers, all the cobblers, all the weavers, and so on. Likewise, all the *kammis* who live in one village, irrespective of their specialized crafts, may be referred to as a *biraderi,* as may all the *kammis* in the whole country. And all those who belong to a village, *zamindars* and *kammis* together, are of one *biraderi.* Thus, the term *biraderi,* which has the primary meaning of patrilineage, may be used to refer to a number of different groupings of people, its specific meaning in each case depending upon the frame of reference and the force of opposition. Thus, the *biraderi* of *zamindars* as a whole may be against the *biraderi* of the *kammis;* or one craft group may be against another; or one village, that is, *zamindars* and *kammis* together, may combine against another village.

In theory, all the members of a *biraderi* (patrilineage) of *zamindar* caste should live in one village or at least in a cluster of neighboring villages. Their common ancestor owned land in that locality, and now all the male descendants, through inheritance, have their share of that land and live in the neighborhood. In actuality, this is not the case. The various branches of one *biraderi* may not be living in the same locality.

In 1887, the construction of irrigation canals in the Punjab brought under cultivation vast stretches of land and new colonies were opened. Some of these arable lands were given by the government as grants to people for their services; some were bought by *zamindars* who needed more land. In this way, the members of a *biraderi* who had acquired land in the new colonies moved away from their original homes. Other members of a *biraderi* who are well educated may also leave the village to enter government service or to follow some career, and they settle in the city.

Yet no matter where they settle, the members of a *biraderi* never sever their connections with their native village. The land they own there, they may not rent to a tenant; if it is cultivated by other members of the *biraderi,* they will get their share. They will sell their fields only as a last resort, if they are in great need of money. Then their *biraderis* have the first option on purchase. If they own a house in the village, they usually ask someone in the village to take care of it; if it is only a house plot, it will remain in their name.

All the members of a *biraderi* of *kammis* should also live in the one village where their ancestors lived and worked. But if there is insufficient work for all of them in one village, some members of the *biraderi* will move to another place where they can find work.

When *zamindars* moved to a new colony or a newly established village, a few *kammis* went along with the *zamindars* and settled there also.

The fact that some of them live at a distance does not affect the close relationships among the members of a *biraderi*. They are always up to date in their information about what is happening in their various branches.

As a group, the *biraderis* are thoroughly involved in family events. Birth, circumcision, marriage, sickness, and death are the occasions when they all come together. Then the presence of the *biraderi* adds to the prestige and enhances the beauty and importance of the occasion. At such times, members of the *biraderi* help to collect the articles necessary for the comfort of the guests, help to entertain the guests, to distribute food, and to see to it that every aspect of the ceremony is well attended to. At the marriage of a poor girl, the members of her *biraderi* who are more well-to-do will give her good clothes and will help in the entertainment of the *barat*, the marriage party, for it enhances the *izzet*, the prestige, of the *biraderi* if the ceremony is done properly.

It also adds to the prestige of an individual and of the *biraderi* as a whole when all its members get along well with one another. Should there be dissension among the members of a *biraderi*, they would try to compose their differences before an important occasion, for all of them should participate in such an event. Failure to do so brings criticism upon the *biraderi*, because they have not been able to find a way to reconcile their quarreling members. Getting along well with their *biraderi* is even more important for those who have sons and daughters of marriageable age. People criticize those who are not on good terms with their *biraderi* and may not want to make a *rishta*, connection through marriage, with such a family.

Although within the *biraderi* certain families may be on more intimate terms with each other than with the group as a whole, all the members show great solidarity when the occasion demands it.

In Mohla, for example, B.A. was the least popular member of his *biraderi*. A *zamindar* from a neighboring village cut down a tree belonging to B.A.; asked why he had done this, the *zamindar* jeered at B.A. B.A. then complained to a member of his *biraderi*, C.H., who was an official in a nearby town. C.H. immediately came to the village, called together several responsible men as well as the offender, and had the whole case discussed in his own presence. The offender admitted his fault and was made to beg B.A.'s pardon.

Although C.H. might neither approve of nor like B.A., he could not tolerate having a member of his *biraderi* humiliated by a member of another *biraderi*, because the insult to B.A. reflected upon the whole *biraderi*. In this connection, a Punjabi would quote the proverb, "Now this is only a footpath, but it may open onto a wide road," which expresses the idea that if a person permits someone to encroach on his honor, no matter how slightly, later this may lead to a more serious offense.

Thus, all the members of a *biraderi* have a feeling of collective honor, the protection of which serves as collective security. In the struggles for power and in quarrels, each *zamindar* will be supported by the members of his own *biraderi*. "He has so many arms to back him up," says a Punjabi proverb; this refers to a person who has many males in the *biraderi* and therefore has power.

The feeling of collective security is even more clearly apparent in the attitude of the *kammis*. A *kammi* may do some wrong, but if he is strongly reprimanded by a *zamindar*, the *kammi's biraderi* will back him up and threaten to leave the village; this act in turn will affect the collective honor of the village. A baker in Mohla, for instance, who was considered to be a good-for-nothing by the members of his *biraderi*, stole some grain from the field of a *zamindar*. The *zamindar's* brother handled the baker rather roughly. Even though the theft was established, the *biraderi* of the baker unanimously supported their member. They stopped heating their ovens and baking the bread, causing everyone great inconvenience, and threatened to leave the village unless the *zamindar* in question apologized to the baker. But this, in turn, would impinge on the honor of *zamindars*. It took lengthy negotiation and careful handling to placate the bakers.

Dadke AND *Nanke:* FATHER'S SIDE AND MOTHER'S SIDE

Learning about different relatives begins early in life. It is customary for a visiting relative to bring sweets or fruit, and as the child is given the delicacy, its grandmother or mother will say repeatedly, "Your mother's brother (or your father's sister, and so forth) has brought these sweets." "For how otherwise," people ask, "is a child to learn about its relatives?"

As the child grows up, he soon learns that the household and the village he lives in are his *dadke*—his father's father's place—while the household and the village he frequently visits with his mother are his *nanke*—the place of his mother's parents. In childhood, boys and girls speak of their *dadke*—parents' home—when they are visiting their *nanke* with their mother. In adulthood, a man refers to *dadke* only to indicate his native place; otherwise he speaks of his home and village.

Dadke is the child's own village, its parents' home. Here is most of the family land and here live most of his *biraderi*, his paternal uncles and cousins, whose number and unity add power and prestige to his family and who are the first to come together and to help on special occasions.

Nanke is cherished throughout life. It is the place where a child is supposed to be treated with great affection and indulgence. From early childhood when one visits one's mother's family one is given much love, and when one returns home one is given sweets and new clothes to take back. When a boy marries, his mother's brother gives him a substantial gift; when a girl marries, part of her dowry comes from her *nanke*. One of the usual questions asked about a marriageable boy or girl is, "Where is his (or her) *nanke?*" For people want to know about the line of the mother as well as about the line of the father.

Peke AND Saure: PATERNAL HOUSE AND SPOUSE'S HOUSE

To a married woman two places are of importance: her *peke,* her paternal household, relatives, and village, and her *saure,* the household, relatives, and village of her husband's family. During the first weeks and even months of her marriage, the bride lives alternately at her *saure* and her *peke.* And later, when she has settled in her husband's village, she visits her parents at least once or twice a year and also goes to her paternal relatives on all important occasions, which breaks the monotony of her life. As she puts it, "If you bake *chapati* (native bread) on one side only, it will burn. You must turn it over."

The doors of her paternal home are always open to her. After the death of her parents, she visits her brothers and so keeps the sense of a continuous relationship. This is continued throughout her life and the lives of her children, for the paternal home is her protection, her security, her place of refuge under all circumstances.

A married woman, when living with her parents-in-law, speaks of her *peke*—the house and village of her parents. But when she visits her *nanke,* then she refers to her parents' home as her *dadke.*

For a married man, the family and the village of his wife are his *saure.* He goes to his *saure* on special occasions and also to inquire about his wife's family, to bring back his wife and children who are visiting there, or to visit her family if he has not been there for a long time. At his *saure* he is treated with special deference and the choicest food is cooked for him. Of a man who sits idle and expects others to serve him, people say, "He behaves like a son-in-law on a visit to his parents-in-law."

Rishtadar OR Saak: RELATIVES

The *rishtadar* or, alternatively, the *saak* is the widest group of people who are recognized as being related to one another. Both of these are terms for a group in which are included consanguinal and affinal [1] relatives: relatives on the father's side and those on the mother's side, the members of the *biraderi,* and relatives by marriage—one's own, those of one's siblings and those of one's children.

When a marriage is being arranged, people say, "We want to make a *rishta* (or a *saak*)," meaning by this that they want to acquire new relatives.

As there is much intermarriage among kin, people are often related to each other in more than one way. This fact is reflected in the way in which kinship terms are used when a relative is addressed by a term which indicates the previous rather than the present relationship. For example, a mother-in-law may be called "father's sister," or a father-in-law may be called "mother's brother," for this was the earlier relationship of the person to the daughter-in-law.

The major responsibilities which kin have to one another are, on the whole, borne by specific clusters of kin—*dadke* and *nanke, peke* and *saure,* and the *biraderi*—and by specific individuals—as, for instance, *phuphi* (father's sister) or *mamuñ* (mother's brother). The *rishtadar,* as such, is a more amorphous group, but one whose members meet on big occasions and among whom the bond of kinship provides a continuing possibility for the development of more active interpersonal relations.

From one point of view, the key figures in the relations among kin are the married women, the married daughters who are the links between two households, between two *biraderi,* between two villages. The daughter married into another village is called *ang* and the daughter's daughter married into another village *prang;*

---

[1] The following are included among the affinal relatives, from the point of view of household: the *peke* of the female head of the household, including her parents, her mother's siblings (and their spouses), her father's siblings (and their spouses), the children of both (and their spouses), and her siblings (and their spouses); the *saure* of the sister of the male head of the household, including her parents-in-law, the siblings of both parents-in-law (and their spouses) and the siblings' children (and their spouses), her husband's siblings (and their spouses) and their children (and their spouses); the *peke* of the son's wife; the *saure* of the daughter.

in the widest sense, all the women born in one village and married into another are "daughters of the village" of their birth. The importance of women as daughters married in other villages is ceremonially recognized, as, for instance, in ceremonies connected with marriage when the family of the bridegroom distributes gifts to married women from the bridegroom's village living in the village of the bride. Certain of the gifts, as also the recipients of the gifts, are called *thehan*, which means "same as daughter" and is derived from *dhi*, daughter.

As married women, daughters—in both the most limited and the widest sense of the term—also have specific responsibilities. One of these is to act as a mediator in disputes or fights within a family, within a *biraderi*, between two *biraderis*, or between people of two villages. In these situations, if no understanding can be reached, the members of a party who want to bring about reconciliation may come to a married daughter and ask her to accompany them to settle the dispute. This mediation by a married daughter is called *meyla*; the expectation is that the married daughter's request will be acceded to by everyone involved.

The working of *meyla* may be illustrated by a case in which a daughter of the village (a woman not actually related to the parties involved) settled a quarrel. In the village of Dhirke, the wives of two *zamindar* brothers did not get along with each other. One day while the two men were working in the fields, Daro, the wife of the younger brother, brought him his lunch and told him that she had had another quarrel with the wife of his older brother. Very annoyed, her husband started to beat her. In the meantime, the wife of the older brother brought him his lunch and told the same story. Her husband cut a sugarcane and began beating her also, but she escaped. Still angry, the older brother then fell on Daro, and the two brothers gave her a good beating. Then Daro took her six-month old baby and went to Samañ, her parents' village. There her father's brother was married to Daro's husband's sister. (This had been a marriage by exchange, *vato sata*; in such marriages it is expected that the two couples will behave alike.) Learning how Daro had come home, the father's brother told his wife to go back to her parents also, because his brother's daughter had not been properly treated in the house of his wife's brother. Daro handed the baby to the woman and said: "Take him back; he belongs to you." The woman left for Dhirke with the baby, but in Dhirke the family had trouble taking care of the baby. The next day two elderly women relatives of Daro's husband came from Dhirke to Mohla and asked the *chowdhrani* of Mohla to come with them to Samañ as *meyla,* to mediate. The *chowdhrani* of Mohla was a daughter of the village of Dhirke, that is, this was her native place. She listened to the explanation of the two women and agreed to go with them to the house of Daro's parents. There the *chowdhrani* gave assurance on behalf of the husband's two women relatives that henceforth Daro would be properly treated in her husband's house and asked Daro's father's brother to take back his wife and to return Daro to her husband. As it is expected that the request of a daughter of the village cannot be refused, Daro's father's brother agreed and the two wives returned, each to her husband.

Obṛ OR *Opra:* NON-KIN

In contrast to the family, the *biraderi,* and the *rishtadar,* everyone else is *obṛ* or, alternatively, *opra,* the people who are not related and consequently who are not kin. A family will say that it has married its son or daughter to an *obṛ,* meaning that the son or daughter has been married into a family with whom there has been no previous connection. As has been indicated, under certain circumstances kinship behavior provides a pattern for the interaction of unrelated people, as when a woman who is the daughter of a village acts in terms of behavior proper to a daughter in the more limited meaning of the term or when two unrelated groups follow the behavior pattern of a true *biraderi,* patrilineage.

To summarize, in this society a man belongs to a certain household, *ghar;* he is a member of his patrilineage, the *biraderi; dadke* is the place of his paternal ancestors, his parents' home, his own home, and the place where his paternal relatives live; he also has a *nanke,* the group of his mother's relatives and the place where they live; and after marriage he establishes connections with the household, the relatives, and the village of his wife, his *saure.*

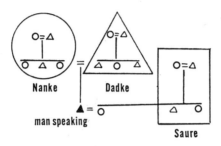

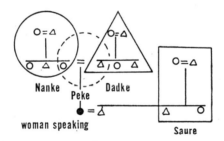

FIGURE 2. KIN GROUPS

A woman after marriage retains her position as the daughter of her paternal home and of her *biraderi,* but she is also included in the household and *biraderi* of her husband; her *nanke* are the household, relatives, and village of her mother's parents; and as a married woman she is the link between her *peke,* her paternal house and relatives and village, and her *saure,* her husband's house, relatives, and village.

Together all these groups of people make up the *rishtadar* or *saak*, the relatives. All other people, outside this widest circle of kin, are *opra* or *obṛ*—strangers—who may be brought into the circle by marriage. In certain circumstances, as is indicated by the extended use of kinship terms (or terms deriving from kinship terms), kinship behavior provides a pattern for relations between people who are not relatives.

IX

Parents and Children: The Years of "Untying the Knots"

Arranging the marriages of their children is a matter of great significance to Punjabi parents and a primary concern in their own lives. To understand fully why this should be so, it is necessary to see what part the marriage of children plays in the lives of the parents and how adults conceptualize the active years of their maturity.

When a married couple assumes the responsibilities of an independent household, this is expressed as "tying the knots around one's neck," which means that one is bound by responsibilities. These responsibilities are mainly to discharge their duty as parents by marrying off their sons and daughters and to maintain good relationships with the members of the various groups with whom they are connected through kinship, work, or by living in the same community. Knots stand for responsibility. (When a barber delivers wedding invitations, he carries with him a long string with as many knots as he has messages to deliver. With each message delivered, he unties a knot, and by the time he has completed his task all the knots are untied.) The years of "untying the knots" are of particular significance to the people because, though they may try hard to discharge their obligations, it is nevertheless within the Divine Power to give or not give them that span of life within which they can achieve their innermost desire, *sadr*, to see their children married and to discharge all their other obligations. Therefore, those who have fulfilled their duties and to whom God gave permission to do so are the fortunate ones at whose death people rejoice.

The years of untying the knots begin not with marriage or with the birth of children, but when a couple has established an independent household. By this time the couple may have grown-up children and may themselves be in their late thirties. Establishing an independent household does not mean that they live in a separate house, apart from the husband's parents, nor does it mean that the husband has received his share of his father's property (though this may also be the case); rather it is the time when the couple assumes the responsibilities of entering into *vartan bhanji* relations by participating independently in important events and carrying on gift exchange independently. Up to this time the husband's parents have carried on gift exchange with the relatives, with the people with whom the family is connected through work, with the neighbors, and with the village as a whole. Having an independent household means that the couple now acts on its own behalf and on behalf of its own children.

For the boy, childhood is a period of preparation when, during frequent visits with his mother to her parents' village—her *dadke* or *peke* and his *nanke*—he develops an affection for his maternal relatives; and living in his father's village—his *dadke*—he learns to value membership in his *biraderi*. By being present at the various kinds of events, he also learns the importance of maintaining proper relations with the people he must some day deal with in everyday life. What is required of him during this preparatory period of life and during his young manhood is that he be a loyal and obedient son.

Similarly the young girl, living at home before marriage, sees how her mother is continually on the alert not to let pass any opportunity to reinforce the relationship between the family and relatives. Then, through her marriage, the girl becomes a link between the families of her parents and her parents-in-law, a connection which is constantly strengthened through gift exchanges between the two families. In the house of her parents-in-law, the young wife is tutored by her mother-in-law in all the details of the *vartan bhanji* transactions between the family of her parents-in-law and their own blood and affinal relatives. She is expected to be an obedient daughter-in-law who, even if her mother-in-law is short-tempered, keeps quiet and evades quarrels. By so doing, she gains the respect and affection of her husband's relatives, and they refer to her as *sherif*—noble.

When an elderly couple has discharged all of its worldly obligations, having dealt properly in *vartan bhanji* with relatives and having its children married, it has fulfilled its obligations as members of a kin group, as members of their social group, and as parents. Then they have succeeded in untying the knots and have fulfilled their *sadr*, their innermost desire. Having established their sons so that they can now turn over to them the responsibilities for carrying on *vartan bhanji* and for realizing their aims in life, the elderly parents can enjoy their achievement until death comes. At this time, after they have discharged their social obligations, the parents may realize another *sadr* by going on a pilgrimage to Mecca. When death comes to such a couple, it is an occasion for rejoicing, for not many people live long enough to realize their *sadr* —to be carried to the grave on the shoulders of married sons and sons-in-law and to leave grandchildren to carry on the line.

At the death of a person who has fulfilled his life tasks and who has lived to old age, *leda* is performed. *Leda* is a ceremony in which the parents of the daughters-in-law bring clothes and give money to the family of the dead, and these, in their turn, distribute clothes among the daughters of the house, lavishly entertain the relatives and friends who have gathered for the occasion, and distribute food and money in the village. *Leda* is performed to honor the deceased—to make him (or her) *vada*, big or great. Honor, so given, reflects on both the ancestors and the descendants of the deceased; for the sons who inherit the material property, this is a

cherished spiritual heritage. The sons of parents who have successfully fulfilled their *sadr* and are so honored are given a good start
in life and are challenged to do as well as their parents have done.

So when a couple forms an independent household, it is entering
into the years of untying the knots and its aim is to complete its
task successfully during its lifetime. The couple knows well what
the responsibilities are that it has undertaken, and it wants to discharge them in a proper way, which will bring social approval. For
social approval brings *izzet*, prestige, and this in turn is the source
of enhanced status, influence, and power. The feeling of *sadr* now
releases and channels the couple's activities toward the goal of
fulfilling its responsibilities.

One aspect of these responsibilities is the maintenance of good
relations with relatives and also with the people one has to deal
with throughout life. So, for instance, it is the duty of the couple
to continue the existence of the *ghar*, the paternal house, to which
the married daughters look for support and for the maintenance of
their own *izzet*, prestige. Good relationships are also built up by
dealing well in *vartan bhanji*, by participating in other people's
joys and sorrows, and by being always fair in this lifelong give and
take. On all occasions, the proper conduct of affairs brings *izzet* to
the family, and so helps the couple to achieve its *sadr*.

However, the primary responsibility of the couple is to fulfill its
parental duty of seeing that its children are married. This is the
essence of its *sadr*, and its fulfillment means the completion of their
main life task. Should they be unable to carry out this parental
duty, it would be a source of grief to them and to their children.
Later, after their death, when the older children give the younger
ones in marriage, they weep at the wedding. They grieve for the
parents who died without realizing their *sadr*, and they weep for
their siblings, who have not realized their *sadr* to be married off by
the parents.

Time is all important for the parents. To carry out their responsibilities during their lifetime, they must see their children married

in good time. Parents begin to consider the problems of a boy's marriage seriously when he is seventeen or eighteen years old; a girl should marry between the ages of fifteen and twenty. Parents whose children are not married at the proper age are regarded as negligent and incapable in the performance of their duties, and this reflects badly on their *izzet*. Consequently, parents try to find a suitable match as soon as possible, and if they are not in a position to undertake the expenses of marriage and its attendant ceremonies, they are likely to borrow money or to resort to one of the alternate, less desirable forms of marriage.

As it is difficult for poor parents to find a bride for their son, they may give a daughter or a niece in exchange for a bride. This form of marriage is called *vaṭo saṭa*. Whenever it is resorted to, people say that there will be trouble, because if one of the two couples does not get along well, the other couple is expected to behave in like manner.

Yet, however poor they may be, all parents want to perform at least some of the ceremonies connected with marriage, for this is the time when relationships previously built up with kin and non-kin are given concrete expression in *vartan bhanji*, both through the exchange of gifts and through participation in the ceremonies, and when additional *izzet*, prestige, comes to all people concerned. By performing the various ceremonies, parents give their child pleasure and simultaneously build up the child's *izzet* in the house and in the village of the parents-in-law. Therefore, in order to conduct these ceremonies in a manner appropriate to their status—which is measured in terms of the family's position in its own *biraderi*— parents will borrow money. Or, alternatively, a marriage may be arranged in which the family of the boy gives a certain sum of money to the family of the girl. This money is spent on the girl's dowry and on the wedding reception. But even though both families gain *izzet* from the performance of ceremonies, this is the least desired form of marriage; neither the girl's side nor the boy's side is likely to mention that money has been given for the bride.

Among well-to-do families, parents begin to look for a suitable match as soon as they feel they are in a position to undertake the marriage expenses and to dispense the necessary obligations of *vartan bhanji,* which forms so prominent a part of the event, taking into consideration at the same time the fact that the girl has become *jivan,* mature. For the parents of a girl make no less effort than the parents of a boy to find a suitable mate; more often than not it is the girl's side which takes the initial steps and proposes to the boy's side. Sometimes if an opportunity arises to make a particularly suitable match and if the parents are then in a position to carry out the ceremonies, there will be no postponement even though the marriage partners are still too young. Consequently, there are cases of child marriages, in which a girl of ten or less is married to a boy of ten or twelve.

In all forms of marriage, consideration is given to the relative age of the partners as it is felt that they should be close in age. In the case of *vato sata,* an adolescent boy will be given a bride of his own age and his child sister will be married to a boy of her own age. Only in the case of the very poor, who must take advantage of whatever opportunity for marriage arises, are disparities in age disregarded. This is particularly true of the boy's side, who will accept a bride much older than the son. As there are fewer women than men in this group, a girl is very precious among the poor.[1] Child marriages occur in all forms of union, but they are rare among the well-to-do.

In a child marriage, the ceremonies of marriage are performed, the dowry is sent to the girl's parents-in-law, and the bride may visit her parents-in-law just once. Then she usually returns to her parents and the marriage is consummated only after she has passed puberty and is between fifteen and eighteen years old. Meanwhile

---

[1] Although census figures show that there is some disparity between the numbers of men and women in the population, the reasons for this are not known. The writer could find no reason why there should have been fewer girls than boys in the families of the poor; however, the belief that this is so is general.

the child husband visits his wife's family and plays with the boys in her village and with his wife, and friendship grows up between them. In some marriages of this kind, the child bride goes to live with her parents-in-law, and her mother-in-law gradually trains her in the ways of the house. But even in these marriages, sexual life begins only after the girl has passed puberty, that is, when she is fifteen years old or older. (Not age but the girl's physical maturation is the determinant.)

The most important social function of marriage is to form a connection between two families or to renew and strengthen an already existing connection. Neither individual choice nor romantic love is relevant to a marriage arrangement; indeed, love as such is not mentioned in connection with marriage.[2] But every relevant aspect of the relationship must be carefully considered. Parents inquire carefully about the family of a prospective mate for their child; they investigate the other family's status, way of living, prestige in the community, ability to get along well with members of their *biraderi*, and relations within the household. They also want to know about the *nanke*, maternal family, of the prospective mate, for the mother's side is considered to be as important as the father's side. The prospective spouse is regarded primarily as a representative of the family; the only information obtained is about his (or her) age and general appearance. By preference, a couple should be close in age and should be of the same skin shade and approximately the same degree of comeliness.

Marriages are endogamous within the caste. *Zamindar* families find spouses for their children among *zamindars* of their own status; *kammis* marry *kammis*. Among the *kammis*, every craft is endogamous: a baker's son marries a girl of the baker caste and a car-

---

[2] Romantic love is a literary theme, but belongs to a different category of relationships from marriage. Even in the cities, among modern and sophisticated young people—for instance, students who have read European and American novels and have seen many Western films—there is little understanding about what is meant by "romantic love" when applied to themselves and their own feelings.

penter's son marries a girl of the carpenter caste. Children know
the caste they belong to from the time they can speak, and by the
time they are six or seven also know that they will marry within
their own caste.

However, there are some exceptions to the rule of endogamy. The
daughter of a *kammi* may marry the son of a *zamindar*. Or the
daughter of a baker may marry the son of another type of craftsman. But such marriages are disapproved of and are entered into
without parental consent. The couple elopes and takes refuge with
friends in a far-away village.

By preference, marriages are arranged within the kin group;
cross-cousin and parallel-cousin marriages are both common. People say that to marry one's daughter to a stranger is to expose the
shortcomings of the family. However, if no suitable mate can be
found among the relatives, families do marry their children to non-
kin. Then, if the family is pleased with the connection formed by
this marriage, other marriages are likely to follow in order to
strengthen the existing link. Among some families, intermarriage
has taken place for three or four generations. In such interrelated
families it is common for a girl to marry into the family of her
father's sister—for instance, she may marry her father's sister's son,
her paternal cross cousin.

The girl's side is pleased with a marriage connection if the bride
is well treated by her family-in-law and if they deal fairly in *vartan
bhanji*. The boy's side is pleased if the girl brings enough dowry
and is an obedient daughter-in-law and if she continues to bring
the customary presents of clothes for herself, her husband, and the
children each time she visits her paternal home. According to a
Punjabi proverb, a mother-in-law says, "I call that one my daughter-
in-law who gives me things to eat," that is, who brings good things
from her parental home.

For both sides, however, the most important aspect of the relationship is *vartan bhanji*—the exchange of gifts and participation in
important events in both families. On the occasion of a marriage, a

birth, or a death in the boy's family, the parents of the girl (or if her parents are dead, her brothers and their wives) should give the customary gifts and should also be present themselves. Similarly, when a sibling of the girl marries, her parents-in-law should see to it that she, as a married woman, can give such gifts as a sister gives to her siblings, and they themselves should be present at the marriage. If the two families deal fairly in *vartan bhanji*—giving and receiving in accordance with their status and *izzet* and attending the ceremonial events in a proper way—their ties are strengthened, and more marriages follow. This applies both to families who are already related and to those between whom the connection is a new one.

On the other hand, if people are not pleased with their daughter-in-law, even though they may go on dealing in *vartan bhanji* with her family—for they are the *nanke*, mother's relatives, of the grandchildren—they will not favor any more marriages into the same family. However well they may treat their daughter-in-law, the fact that no further marriages take place, though there are possible matches, reflects their discontent. Similarly, even though the girl's family may be displeased with the husband's family, they will nevertheless try to maintain a good relationship through *vartan bhanji*, so as to make her life easier. For both families, it is a matter of *izzet* that a girl should be properly treated by her husband's family and that she should get along well with them.

The establishment of a good relationship between the two families is of the utmost importance for the woman, for she never severs her ties to her own family; from the beginning of her marriage she moves back and forth between the two houses.

Before the marriage, if the couple is already related and the bridegroom has previously visited the village of his prospective parents-in-law, he does not go there from the time of the engagement until the day of the marriage. If he lives in the same village, he will avoid passing the house of his prospective parents-in-law during the same period.

At the time of the marriage, the bride and bridegroom each make three formal visits to the house and village of the respective parents-in-law. The boy comes first as a *laṛa*, bridegroom, with the *barat,* the wedding procession, to fetch his bride. When the bridegroom and *barat* then bring the bride to his house and village, she comes as a *dulin,* one who comes in a *ḍowli,* a palanquin. After one night, she returns to her parents' home with her husband, accompanied by the bride's father, paternal or maternal uncle, or her brother, who come to bring the couple home. This is the bridegroom's second visit, *muklawa,* to his parents-in-law. The couple stays for two or three days. Then the parents of the bridegroom, his paternal or maternal uncle, or his brother come to take the couple back to the husband's house. This is the bride's *muklawa* to her parents-in-law. This time she stays for several days. Then her paternal or maternal uncle (not the same person who came before) comes to bring the couple again to the girl's parents. However, the bridegroom may or may not accompany his wife on this visit; if he goes, this would be his third visit, *tarwianda,* to his parents-in-law. They or she will stay with her parents for a week or more. Toward the end of this visit, either her husband (if he did not accompany her when she came) or some close relative of his (not the same person who came before) will come to bring the bride for her third visit, *tarwianda,* to her parents-in-law. She will stay with them for over a week. Then one of her close relatives will come to take her to her parents to stay for a few months. This time her husband will not accompany her; later he will visit his parents-in-law occasionally. After several months the husband or one of his close relatives will bring the wife back to her parents-in-law. This time she settles down in her new home. Her mother-in-law tells her to cook *khichṛi,* a dish made with rice and lentils; this is the signal that she is expected to take up her household duties.[3] Thus, the woman's lifelong alternation between her *peke* and her *saure* is set in motion.

---

[3] The bride is told to cook *khichṛi* either on her third visit to her parents-in-law or after she has settled down in her new home.

During this period of visits, each time the young wife leaves her parental home she is given gifts of clothes, as are also her husband and any of his relatives who come to accompany her back to her married home. And every time she visits back and forth, large quantities of sweets are sent by her parents to her parents-in-law and by her parents-in-law to her parents; these sweets are distributed in the villages.

Finally, after the prolonged stay with her parents, the bride settles down in her husband's home. However, she visits her parents at least twice a year and also takes part in all important family events there. Later she takes her children with her. So much a part of the life of a family and of a village are a woman's visits to her *peke* and *saure*, that children rocking back and forth in a swing will chant in rhythmic accompaniment to the motion, "Going to your *saure*, coming back to your *peke*."

A woman's connection with her father's house is her life artery, through which flow the presents which bring her *izzet* among her family-in-law and which, even more, contribute to the *izzet* of her parents. Her parental house is always open to her, and she can turn to it at all times. After her parents have died, her brothers and their wives will continue the tradition of the parental house, the *ghar*, for it enhances their own *izzet* to respect their sister, who is a *phuphi*, paternal aunt, of their children.

A *phuphi* has a special position in the household of her brother. From childhood, a sister and a brother are considered to be very close. A boy receives his first *pagri*, turban, from his married sister. (If he does not have an older sister, then his father's sister will give it to him.) The *pagri* is a symbol of honor, and proper behavior between a brother and a sister enhances the honor, *izzet*, of both. For a sister, a brother is the person who, if the father is not living, is responsible for arranging her marriage and for continuing the gift giving though which she and her children acquire *izzet*. She is the person for whom the brother feels responsible and who is the source of his *izzet*, as he fulfills his duties to her and to her children, for by giving gifts and by making his sister and her children always feel welcome, he and the *ghar* which he represents gain in *izzet*. A brother occupies the foremost place in a woman's thoughts; at his death, she will be the one most grieved. To her children, he is a loving *mamuñ*, maternal uncle; to his children she is a *phuphi*—the very sound of this word brings to people's minds someone much respected and cherished. A man who has no sister will feel deeply the lack of that particular relationship, and his children will always have a *sadr*, an unfulfilled desire, for a *phuphi*.

Phuphi is the person who cares genuinely for her brother's children, and it is to her they turn in times of difficulty. Whenever an important decision must be made, *phuphi* is consulted and her opinion respected. On her visits home, if her brother has died, she may refuse to accept the gifts to which she is entitled as a daughter of the house because her nephews are young and she does not wish them to spend money on her. However, there will be times when she does accept the gifts, both to increase the *izzet* of her father's house and to build up her own *izzet* among the wives of her husband's brothers. In such situations, despite the expectation that one always gives to and never receives from a daughter of the house, the *phuphi* will find ways of giving more presents to the sons and daughters of her deceased brother than she has received from them, for she wishes to be a very "good and loyal daughter of the house."

Close as a woman is to her brothers, her relationships with her brothers' households depend largely upon their wives; consequently, she may favor and be favored by the family of one of her brothers and be less close to the others. If the children of one of her brothers do not have a *mamuñ* (for instance, if their mother has lost her brothers), and if there is nobody to represent the *nanke* when these children marry, a sister will see to it that her husband fills the gap; he, the *phuphar*, father's sister's husband, will fulfill the function and make up for the missing maternal relatives.

When a woman is widowed, the possibilities open to her depend on the stage of her life, on whether or not she has children—especially sons—on her relationship to her husband's family, and on conditions in her paternal home. A woman who is widowed late in life may be the head of her household and have grown-up sons. If she is young and has children, her parents-in-law may think it best for her to marry a younger brother of her late husband; if she agrees, she will become his second wife. But if she is young and has no sons to inherit the land (providing she is of the *zamindar* caste), if she has found her mother-in-law difficult to get along with and her brothers and parents, if they are alive, have found *vartan bhanji* dealings with the family of her parents-in-law unsatisfactory, then her family would feel that there was no point in continuing the relationship and would bring their widowed daughter or sister back home with them. They would not claim back the dowry—the clothes, furniture, and buffaloes—she had taken with her, for that is a matter of her parents' *izzet*. A widow with daughters may take them home with her. But sometimes the husband's family will not let the children leave; if there are daughters, they will be engaged to sons of the dead father's brothers, and the widow will be allowed to leave alone. In other circumstances, for example, where the husband's family is considerate, the widow will remain, for it is the family's *izzet* to continue to maintain a widowed daughter-in-law in its household.

A widow may go to live with her parents, if they are alive. Or she may go to live with her brother, but she must be on good terms with his wife. Otherwise life will not be easy for her. Yet it is the *izzet* of her brother and his family to treat her well and to take good care of her. She may also remarry, in which case the children may or may not go with her. However, it is the *izzet* of her brothers not to have their widowed sister remarry, for they should be able to provide for her.

The marriage of a widow is performed very inconspicuously. The ceremony takes place at night and only a few people are present to hear the *imam* read the *nikah,* marriage contract. Asked why the ceremony takes place at night and why so little is said about it, the village women would reply, "It is a shame for a widow to remarry."

A woman's relationship with her parental house is that of a daughter, a sister, and, later, a paternal aunt. Yet, whatever gifts she receives, she receives always as the daughter of the house. The head of the *ghar* who gives may be much younger than the woman who receives as the daughter; here *ghar* stands for the line of ancestors with whom the receiver is connected.

To be balanced, a family should have both daughters and sons for the perfect functioning of this family system in which one continually gives to daughters and receives from daughters-in-law by way of sons.

Families who lack either sons or daughters or who have no children cannot participate fully as members of their kin group. Although they participate in the various ceremonies of their kin and deal in *vartan bhanji,* and although their kindred are considerate of their incompleteness, yet they cannot actually experience the joy of the whole ceremony and must continually adjust themselves to what is lacking. A man who has no son may treat his sister's son as his own; the young man will live for some time in the village of his maternal uncle and may marry his cross cousin. A childless family may adopt a girl, given to them by relatives who have many children. But to participate fully, a family should have both sons and daughters. Participation means that a family meets with relatives on appropriate occasions and engages in all the appropriate gift exchanges. Indeed, relationships with all those whom one regards as kin, whether through blood or marriage, can be kept alive only as long as they are kept active. In this connection, the Punjabi quote the following proverb: "A well is a well as long as it works; relatives are relatives as long as they meet." And then they will explain that if a well is not used, it fills with sand and falls into disrepair and finally cannot be called a well; in like manner, unless relatives meet and share in one another's troubles and joys they grow apart and cannot be called relatives.

Meetings of relatives do not take place at random; rather there are certain important events in the lives of family members—birth, the circumcision of a son, marriage, departure for a pilgrimage, sickness, and death—in which all the relatives should take part. But full participation depends not only on their presence at events but also on their dealing in *vartan bhanji*, which is the outstanding part of the attendant ceremonies. Although everyone is involved in *vartan bhanji*, the central figure is the daughter, so that in one sense one may say that a daughter is as crucial to *vartan bhanji* as *vartan bhanji* is to the whole of the traditional culture.

Nevertheless, it is equally important for a family to have sons, because sons continue the ancestral line, inherit the land (if they are *zamindars*) or follow the father's craft (if they are *kammis*), and maintain the tradition of the *ghar*, the parental household on which their sisters depend. Unless there is a son, a family cannot have the ceremony of receiving *leda* at the death of an old person who has completed his (or her) life task. *Leda* honors the dead and the living in both families; those who bring and those who receive *leda* gain much *izzet*.

Households in which there are both sons and daughters are fortunate. They will give to their daughters and they will receive through their daughters-in-law, who are the daughters of other families, and so the equilibrium is maintained.

Part II. *Vartan Bhanji*

X

The Meaning of *Vartan Bhanji*

Vartan bhanji is a mechanism of gift exchange widely practiced in the Punjab. The term means an exchange of gifts and also refers to gifts so exchanged; likewise it denotes the relationship between people established through this exchange. Literally, *vartan bhanji* means "dealing in sweets," and it has the extended meaning of "dealing in relationships." In Punjabi, the verb *vartna* means "to deal," and its derivative *vartan* means "dealing." *Bhanji* means "sweets," and it is also used with the meaning of "relationship." *Vartan bhanji* involves an exchange of sweets, fruit, food, money, and yard goods for clothes; extending beyond material things, it includes the exchange of favors, services, like treatment, entertainment, and participation in ceremonial events. In its operation this mechanism of exchange involves a wide range of relationships among the various groups who make up this society. It is of vital importance to people as a means of achieving *izzet*, prestige.

Although *vartan bhanji* is basically a relationship developing out of gift exchange, the same term is applied to another kind of relationship in which no gifts need be exchanged, but in which two parties—two individuals, two families, two villages—feel free to ask favors of each other. This type of relationship goes beyond mere acquaintanceship as it implies a certain degree of friendliness and of rapport, and a willingness to ask for and to grant favors. So, for instance, if a *zamindar* is in need of *mang*, collective labor, he may ask his friend in another village with whom he has a relationship involving exchange of favors to provide him with extra help. In this case, he puts himself under obligation to the person with whom he is on *vartan bhanji* terms; his friend, in turn, puts himself under obligation to all the people who joined the *mang* at his request.

In popular usage, *vartan bhanji* may have various meanings. It may mean the relationship, or the way of dealing, or the articles of exchange, or behavior on certain occasions. So, for example, a woman may say, "We are on *vartan bhanji*," or "We have *vartan bhanji*," meaning that her family has a gift exchange relationship with another family. Or someone may say, "Her *vartan bhanji* is very good," in the sense that she deals fairly and acts according to the unwritten but well-known rules of this relationship. Again, a woman may show off the gifts she has received on some occasion and say that they are *vartan bhanji,* meaning that these were received in gift exchange and must be reciprocated. Or a woman may weep more at one funeral than at another and say that this was *vartan bhanji,* meaning that she shed more tears because of the closer degree of *vartan bhanji* between her household and the one where she wept more.

Vartan bhanji operates on two bases. The first is the daughter's right in her parents' home. The second is the relationship established through the exchange of gifts and favors.

A daughter's right in her parents' home is constantly validated through the gifts she receives on her visits and on all the major occasions celebrated in her own or in her father's household. Although what she receives is her right and is not *vartan bhanji,* yet this very right serves as a pattern for the operation of *vartan bhanji.* On ceremonial occasions, when a family celebrates an event by giving presents to a number of women, they first define the relationship between themselves and each woman who is to receive a gift and then they equate this relationship to that of a "daughter." In her capacity as a daughter, the woman who represents her household receives gifts, and through her other members of the household may also be recipients. For instance, any woman of the *biraderi,* the patrilineage, if she is of the same generation as the head of the house, will be equated with a sister and so will be treated as a daughter of the house. On this basis, the family carries on *vartan bhanji* with members of its *biraderi,* affinal relatives, and close friends.

The second basis for *vartan bhanji* is the relationship which is established through the exchange of sweets, foods, and favors. On a ceremonial occasion, a household celebrates the event by distributing food and sweets in the village; by doing so, it emphasizes its relationship with the village community as a whole. It is on the basis of this relationship that a household can deal with the people beyond its immediate circle of relatives and friends and can have *vartan bhanji* with the village as a whole. On the same basis, a village as a whole can have *vartan bhanji* with other villages.

Vartan bhanji transactions do not take place at random, but on specific ceremonial occasions. The principal occasions on which gift exchanges take place are birth, the circumcision of a son, marriage, and the death of an old person. Once a *vartan bhanji* relationship has been established there are a number of other occasions when gifts may be given and received; these include times of sickness and convalescence, departure for a pilgrimage to Mecca, and, lately, departure abroad for education. On all such occasions sweets, food, clothing, and money are the counters in the gift exchange, the kind and amount of each depending upon the particular event and the scale of the *vartan bhanji* relationship.

For families, particularly for the women, *vartan bhanji* is like an exciting game which people play with absorbing interest and zeal. They can conduct exchange on any scale by expanding the circle of people with whom they deal, but they must be careful to maintain the pace for everything must be reciprocated and the dealings should be carried on at a level appropriate to one's status. The gain in this game is *izzet,* prestige.

XI

The Daughter's Role

It has already been said that the daughter is crucial to *vartan bhanji*. She is at the core of the exchange, for she is the figure through whom and in whom all the relationships and all the dealings in *vartan bhanji* among kin are expressed and her special role makes it possible for the exchange to be extended and to continue indefinitely.

In *vartan bhanji* a daughter's role is to receive, and it is she who receives on all occasions. So at the marriage of a son, the family gives away cloth for outfits and quantities of sweets; the main recipients are the daughters. At the marriage of a daughter, the relatives and friends bring gifts; the recipient is the daughter, the bride. The occasion of a boy's marriage is the proper occasion for a family to give away gifts. Relatives and friends do not bring gifts, but may give the bridegroom money, *selami,* to welcome him as a bridegroom; his married sisters bring clothes for him, but these are only a token of their close relationship, for they expect to be given things many times the value of what they have brought. When the groom's family distributes gifts, the daughters—that is, the sisters and paternal aunts of the boy—will receive the most. But in addition to giving to their own daughters, the family gives clothes and sweets to a large group of women who attend the wedding. In giving to these women, the main rule observed is that all these women receive as *ghar di dhi,* daughters of the house. If the house of marriage wishes to carry on *vartan bhanji* on a large scale, the circle of women to whom gifts are given will be enlarged by extending to its members the term *ghar di dhi,* which makes them eligible to receive. On a parallel occasion—that is, at the marriage of a son—the families of these women will reciprocate with those from whom on this occasion they have received.

In working out such extensions it may be said, for instance, that a younger brother's wife is my sister, therefore she is a daughter of the house; a friend is my brother, therefore his wife is my sister and is a daughter of the house; my brother's daughter and daughter-in-law are my daughters; my daughter's sister-in-law is her sister, and therefore my daughter. In this way, nieces, cousins, the daughters of sons and daughters, sisters-in-law, all may be included in the category of daughter of the house, and so be entitled to receive presents.

In fact, when a family wishes to give away many presents, it observes the fundamental rule of giving: "For giving is like the flow of water which goes from the high level to the low, from the rich to the poor, from the older to the younger." Where status and age are equal, then the kinship position will be taken into account. So, for instance, if a woman recipient is older in age than the donors, then her relationship to the family is reduced to the least common denominator in *vartan bhanji* and she is treated as a daughter of the house.

To give to the daughter of a family is essential. If the family of a bridegroom wants to express a greater intimacy with certain relatives it may, in addition, give clothes to her whole family, including the men.

At the marriage of a son, the family of the bridegroom also receives presents, but the central figure is still the daughter. At her son's wedding, a woman receives presents of clothes for herself from her parents as their daughter, and the bridegroom receives a sum of money or a gift from his *nanke,* maternal family, as the son of their daughter. The man is more or less a neutral figure throughout these dealings. The groom's sisters, his paternal aunts, and the daughters of the house receive gifts from the paternal home as daughters; and the bride brings a dowry to his family, a portion of which she has received from her *nanke* as its daughter's daughter and the rest of which she has received from her parents as their daughter.

Similarly, when a man's son is born or is circumcised, the daughters are the main recipients of gifts. The man's sister or his father's brother's daughter will bring a present for the child and will expect to be given much more in return. Should she not be satisfied with the gift, she may not accept it, saying: "A son is born to my brother (or cousin). It is an occasion for rejoicing, and I must get a good suit of clothes, not an inferior one." At the same time the mother of the newborn receives presents from her parents as their daughter.

At the marriage of its daughter, a family receives from relatives and friends, with whom it is on *vartan bhanji* terms, clothes for the bride and an amount of sweets equivalent to what in the past it has given at the weddings of their daughters. On this occasion, the women who, at the marriages of their own daughters, had received gifts as daughters of the house, will bring clothes for the bride as her "elder sisters," as her paternal and maternal aunts, and as the wives of her paternal and maternal uncles, and so on. The mother of the bride knows exactly what to expect, for she knows well—and has often described—the quantity and quality of the clothes she has given away to the families with whom she deals in *vartan bhanji.*

To have a daughter is important, because the marriage of a daughter is the occasion for the family on which they can enjoy the reward of their longstanding relations with others. What they receive now is the sum total of what they have given away to their relatives and friends at the marriages of their daughters; now everything comes back. A family without daughters is denied this joy, and although it scrupulously enters *vartan bhanji*—giving the traditional welcome money, *selami*, to the bride and bringing clothes for her—it does so halfheartedly for there is no real excitement to look forward to. Even though it will receive back on various occasions what it has given, the deep satisfaction attached to this particular event is missing. Furthermore, though a woman who does not have a daughter will be given clothes (or else these will be given to her daughter-in-law) on appropriate occasions, nevertheless this act of receiving the gift will not carry with it the amount of *izzet* which a family gains and enjoys at the marriage of its own daughter through receiving gifts at that time from relatives and friends with whom it is dealing in *vartan bhanji*.

At the marriage of a son, the family gives gifts and gains *izzet*. And at the marriage of a daughter, the family receives gifts and again gains *izzet*. The number and quality of the gifts given and received are indications of the family's knowledge and ability in dealing with people and provide an index of its status, influence, and power and of the breadth of its social circle—all of which means *izzet*. On all such occasions daughters are crucial to the exchange and hence to the acquisition of *izzet*.

It has been mentioned that the married daughter is also very important in making and keeping alive connections between villages. Her key position is ceremonially recognized at the time of a marriage when the family of the bridegroom sends presents with the *barat*, the group of men who comes with the bridegroom to fetch the bride in her village. The bridegroom and the *barat* come bringing gifts for the bride, and the principal ceremonies are those centering on the bride and bridegroom. But in addition, the *barat* brings gifts and may perform ceremonies in the bride's village honoring married daughters and the bride's village as a whole. Through these ceremonies and the gifts presented, the family of the bridegroom establishes—or strengthens and renews—relationships not only with the family of the bride but also with certain households in her village, and his village establishes a relationship with her village as a whole and with a number of villages in the neighborhood.

This is done by giving gifts, *thehan*, by the giving of money as *chul,* and by the performance of the ceremony of *ratha chari.* For example, M.S., a *zamindar* of Mohla, was arranging the marriage of his sister. Soon after the *barat* arrived in Mohla the boy's side sent presents to some women in this village who belonged to the same subcaste, in this case Chatha, as the bridegroom, and to others who came from his village and were married in Mohla. Among the latter group were both *zamindar* and *kammi* women. Each woman received as a gift a copper plate filled with sweets and some money, the amount varying from 2, 5, 11, 21, up to 101 rupees. (In making this gift, some families send the same amount to all women while others send more to those whom they regard as important to themselves.)

This gift is called *thehan,* a word which derives from *dhi,* daughter, and has the same meaning as daughter; the woman who receives the gift is also called *thehan.* The gift recognizes the recipient as a daughter and by giving it the bridegroom's family honors the daughters of their subcaste and of their village who live in the bride's village. The woman who receives *thehan* keeps the plate and the sweets and some of the money (at least one or two rupees, at most five rupees, depending on the scale on which the bridegroom's family is dealing). Later on the same day, when the bridegroom receives *selami,* money given to "welcome" him, all the *thehan* go to the bride's house and give him *selami* and *sagan.*[1] Those who are much older than he give him *selami* as father's sisters and the others as his sisters. By giving *selami,* these women honor the bride's family whose son-in-law the young man has become, and thus establish *vartan bhanji* with them. The bridegroom accepts the *sagan* but returns the *selami,* for *thehans* are daughters.

On the same occasion, while the *barat* is in the village of the

---

[1] *Sagan* consists of a small amount of coconut, almonds, and raisins or some sweets given as a symbol of relationship to a bride or bridegroom when he or she comes for the first time to the house of his spouse's relatives. *Sagan* also is given to a child the first time it comes to the house of a family with whom the parents have *vartan bhanji.*

bride, the bridegroom's family may further strengthen the ties between its own village and that of the bride as a whole by distributing money to all the households of *kammis* there.

For example, at the marriage of R.B., a sister of the *chowdhri*
of Mohla, while the *barat* was in the bride's village, the bridegroom's father distributed 10 rupees to each *kammi* household.
This money is called *chul,* which means "the hearth." Through the
distribution of *chul* both families are honored—the bridegroom's
and the bride's—and gain in prestige, and so do the villages of the
donor and the recipients.

Likewise on the occasion of the coming of the *barat* the bridegroom's family may also perform the ceremony of *ratha chari,*
which means "knightly gesture," and by so doing they honor the
daughters and daughters' daughters of other villages who are married into the bridegroom's village (that is, the daughters-in-law in
his village).

For example, at the marriage of the sister of A.M., a *zamindar*
of Mohla, on the morning after the arrival of the *barat,* all the male
guests were assembled at the men's guest house. Then the bridegroom's maternal uncle, some of his *biraderi,* and the *mirasi,* village
bard, of Mitha Chak—the bridegroom's village—seated themselves
on the roof of the veranda of the guest house. Below in the courtyard were gathered also the *mirasis* of the neighboring villages.
The *mirasi* of Mitha Chak called the names of the villages in the
area one by one. The *mirasi* of the village named, if he was present,
stepped up and said: "I am the *mirasi* of ——," naming the village.
He then received two rupees, the basic amount given to each. But
some *mirasi* received more if they could claim that they had *ang*
or *prang,* married daughters or daughters' daughters from their
village living in Mitha Chak. For each daughter of his village the
mirasi received one rupee and for each daughter's daughter half
a rupee. The *mirasi* of Mitha Chak knew well all the *angs* and
prangs living in his village and the names of the villages from
which they and their mothers came. Reciprocally, the *mirasis* from

other villages knew which of their daughters and daughters' daughters were married in Mitha Chak.

By distributing this money, the family of the bridegroom honors the daughters of other villages who are married in the bridegroom's village and consequently establishes—or strengthens and renews— relations between its own and these other villages. The family's own village gains much *izzet* and becomes an outstanding village, a *ṭika* village (a *ṭika* is a gold ornament worn on the forehead).

Thus, at a marriage, at that stage where the bridegroom's family is honoring the bride's family in her own village, the performance of ceremonies honoring a true daughter (the bride as a daughter of her family and as the daughter-in-law, *nuh*, of the bridegroom's family) sets off other ceremonies in which daughters, more broadly defined, and the village itself are honored. These ceremonies not only bring *izzet* to all those concerned but also initiate or strengthen *vartan bhanji* relations.

Nevertheless, important as is the role of the daughter in the exchange of gifts, those gifts that are given to a true daughter are not *vartan bhanji*. They are considered to be "the daughter's right," and therefore, looked at in this way, are not to be reciprocated and are not part of the system of exchange. It is the gifts which are given to the daughters of a house, the daughters of a subcaste, the daughters of a village—to daughters in extended meanings of the term—that must be reciprocated, for these are *vartan bhanji*. Thus, the giving to the true daughters sets the pattern for the main recipients of the gifts, but the pattern of reciprocal giving is set primarily by relations with the *ghar di dhi*, the daughters of the house, and then is extended to daughters otherwise defined.

It should be noted, however, that there is one modification of the rule that daughters receive but do not reciprocate. One of the basic rules of *vartan bhanji* is that no one comes empty-handed and no one goes away empty-handed.[2] One gives and one receives. This

---

[2] See Chapter XIII for a discussion of the rules of *vartan bhanji*.

applies to daughters and to others to whom gifts are given, but the ratio of giving and receiving is very different.

In *vartan bhanji*, as will be shown, the exchange of gifts is kept close to balance in the long run, but in the case of a true daughter, the ratio of gifts given to her and of those received from her by her parents' household is approximately ten to one. That is, parents expect to give about ten times as much as they may expect to receive from their married daughter's household.

For example, at the marriage of a daughter's daughter, the maternal grandparents may take clothes and ornaments worth 1,000 rupees as presents for the bride and her mother (their granddaughter and daughter), and they may expect to return home bringing presents worth approximately 100 rupees.[3] However, if the relationship between the parents and the daughter and her family-in-law is a very good one, then the ratio may be about eight to one. That is, the daughter's parents will be given more presents than custom demands. Thus, in a very modified way, the wider pattern of *vartan bhanji* is reflected in the relations between a true daughter and her family in so far as intimacy and warmth of feeling should be expressed in the manner of giving.

[3] See also Chapter XIII, in which the point is made that the present given and the present received on one occasion are not, in fact, one transaction but aspects of two different transactions. However, the disproportion between what a daughter gives and what she receives as her right holds throughout in her case.

XII

The Groups Involved

The people who deal in *vartan bhanji* may be grouped as follows:

1. Relatives, blood and affinal.
2. Friends.
3. Members of the same caste, for example, a *zamindar* who has *vartan bhanji* relations with other *zamindars* in his own or in other villages, or a *kammi* (such as a barber) who has *vartan bhanji* relations with other *kammis* of his caste (barbers) in his own or in other villages.
4. Members of different castes, for example, a *zamindar* who has *vartan bhanji* with a *kammi,* and vice versa, or a *kammi* (such as a barber) who deals with *kammis* of other castes (with a carpenter, a blacksmith, and so on).
5. Neighbors.
6. The villagers as a whole.
7. A village that has *vartan bhanji* with another village.

Vartan bhanji is usually carried on between households. It is the married woman, especially the oldest woman in a household, who takes the active, leading part in the dealings both through the exchange of gifts and through attendance at important events where she represents her household. An unmarried girl does not deal in *vartan bhanji,* for it is her mother who represents the household. A daughter-in-law is introduced gradually into *vartan bhanji* by her mother-in-law, who will begin to send her to attend ceremonies and on these occasions she will represent the household. A woman who represents a household has *vartan bhanji* with a number of families in the village and outside; these are primarily relatives, blood and affinal, and friends with whom the family is on intimate terms. Beyond this circle are the neighbors, the households with whom a family is connected through work—the *seypis*—people who live in the same village or, if the village is large (some villages have a population from 2,000 to 5,000), those who live on the same street or block, and some families in neighboring villages.

A *zamindar* family has *vartan bhanji* with all the groups listed above. With each of these groups, *vartan bhanji* is conducted on a different scale. With the kin group and with some close friends, *vartan bhanji* is carried on in its fullest sense: an extensive exchange of gifts and full participation in all ceremonial occasions. This group, taken as a whole, constitutes the social circle of the family—including all those on whom the family can rely to participate in all events and to bring the customary gifts as well, because the family fully reciprocates. A person who does not deal in *vartan bhanji* with his (or her) relatives may be entirely isolated.

A second group with whom a *zamindar* deals is that of the *ghar da kammi*, the *kammis* of the house. The basis of their close relations, which may have continued for several generations, is reciprocity—the services rendered by the *kammis* and the protection, payments, and support given by the *zamindar*. In this relationship, *vartan bhanji* is not maintained on the full basis of gift exchange and participation in big events.

The other *zamindars* in the village and in neighboring villages, who are not kin, and the *kammis*, who are not *ghar da kammi* of the family but have *vartan bhanji* with certain *zamindar* families, participate only to a limited degree in the various ceremonies. They are not part of the *meylis*, the group of relatives and friends who are the wedding guests and who participate fully in all the stages of the occasion, of bringing sweets and giving clothes and money and later receiving sweets and clothes from the family.

A *kammi* household deals in *vartan bhanji* with the various groups also—the *biraderi,* maternal relatives, affinal relatives (all of whom are of the same craft and hence belong to the same caste), the *zamindars* and the *kammis* with whom it has *seyp,* other *zamindars* and *kammis* of different crafts in the village with whom it is on friendly terms, with most other *kammis* in the village and a few in neighboring villages.

For example, at the wedding of a baker in Mohla, the entries in the family register, called *vehi*—in which are recorded the names of the people present and the amounts of money and articles given by them on this and other occasions—indicated the range of people with whom this *kammi* family deals in *vartan bhanji*: members of the *biraderi* (all bakers), other relatives, a few *zamindars, kammis* of other castes (weavers, cobblers, carpenters), and, in addition, a few Sikhs and Hindus with whom the bakers had been dealing prior to Partition.[1]

Relatives form the main group with whom a family has *vartan bhanji.* Among the relatives, a woman who represents a household deals with the following: her husband's married sisters and brothers and their parents-in-law; her husband's *biraderi* (which is also her own after her marriage); her *peke*—her married sisters and brothers and their parents-in-law—and the *biraderi* of her parents; the several sets of parents-in-law of her married sons and daughters. There is no *vartan bhanji* between parents and children, but a family deals in *vartan bhanji* with the children's parents-in-law.

However, a family does not deal with all the possible relatives and, among those with whom it does deal, the degree of *vartan bhanji* depends upon the intimacy existing between two households. With some relatives, *vartan bhanji* may be restricted to attendance at major events, such as a marriage or the death of an old person; with others, every event—sickness, birth, circumcision, and so forth—is considered an occasion for meeting and exchanging

---

[1] See Appendix III, *Vehi:* The Family Register, in which a page is reproduced from a *vehi* of a *kammi* family.

gifts, but there may be visiting back and forth between such households at any time.

For example, Bebeji (the mother of the *chowdhri* of Mohla, whom most of the village people call *bebeji*, mother) has a number of relatives with whom she deals, but as she says: "There is a difference and there is a difference in *vartan bhanji*." Among all the relatives, her closest and warmest relationship is with the *phuphi* of the house, her late husband's sister; next to her are the parents of her daughter-in-law and the widow of her eldest son. With the other relatives, Bebeji maintains *vartan bhanji* to varying degree.

Such are the subtle differences that depend primarily upon intimacy, on the one hand, and the desire to give or to receive *izzet*, prestige, on the other. In a broader sense, the people with whom a family deals in *vartan bhanji* and the types of transaction can be divided into two broad categories: first, relatives and very intimate friends with whom are exchanged sweets, fruits, food, yard goods, money, sometimes a buffalo or a horse, and golden ornaments; and second, the unrelated people with whom lesser exchanges are made of sweets, fruit, food, and money.

So, for example, Bebeji discusses with the author the dealings which the family of the *chowdhri* of Mohla has with Mand, a *zamindar* in a neighboring village. These two families are on friendly but not intimate terms and their *vartan bhanji* relation fits into the second category.

Bebeji: We have "little" *vartan bhanji* with Mand. On the circumcision of his children I sent 5 rupees and two *seers* of sugar (one *seer* equals two pounds). When Perwez and Gul[2] were circumcised, Mand sent eight *seers* of rice, two *seers* of sugar, and 10 rupees. I took 5 rupees and sent back the rest of the money. The point is that the sugar and money were mine and only the rice was his.[3] On the occasion of the marriage of Mand's son I sent

[2] Bebeji's son's sons.
[3] That is, Mand had a balance of eight *seers* of rice to his credit.

eight *seers* of rice, 5 rupees and two *seers* of sugar. So his rice was returned and now he had 5 rupees and two *seers* of sugar which he owed us. Now again, on the marriage of his daughters, F.A.[4] gave 10 rupees. So we have with them 15 rupees, and two *seers* of sugar. On the marriage of Z.[5] or of F.A., Mand will give selami[6] or neondra.[7] That is the way *vartan bhanji* goes.

Z.E.: What if you want to stop *vartan bhanji*?

Bebeji: I will send a man to ask back the 15 rupees and two *seers* of sugar, and *vartan bhanji* will be finished.

Z.E.: What about the food he sent on the marriages of his sons and daughter?

Bejebi: When Z. marries, we'll send him food during the day and at night. After all, it is *vartan bhanji*. What you owe him, you still owe; even if you stopped dealing, you would have to repay.

Bebeji speaks also of the types of things exchanged.

Bebeji: At the circumcision of Gul and Perwez, people brought gur,[8] rice, refined sugar, seviyañ,[9] money. In return we put panjiri[10] in the vessels of those who brought rice, sugar, gur, and so on, but did not give anything to those who gave money. To them we will give money on a like occasion. Badro, the baker, gave 10 rupees at that time; two years later, when Badro's little son was brought to this house for the first time, we gave him sagan[11] and 5 rupees. Those who give money receive back money. That is *vartan bhanji*.

Z.E.: If a man has no children, how will people reciprocate?

---

[4] Bebeji's son, the *chowdhri* of Mohla.

[5] Bebeji's youngest, unmarried daughter.

[6] "Welcoming" money given to a bride or bridegroom.

[7] Money given to the parents of the bridegroom by those on *vartan bhanji* with them.

[8] Brown sugar.

[9] Vermicelli.

[10] Sweets made of *gur*, flour, and *ghi*.

[11] See Chapter XI, footnote 1.

Bebeji: He will carry on *vartan bhanji.* People will find a way to give him back.

The difference between the two categories of people and of *vartan bhanji* gifts is indicated also by actual behavior on ceremonial occasions. So, for example, at the birth of a child—especially a son—two forms of notification are used. To the *nanke,* the child's *phuphi,* and the father's *phuphi,* the family may send a messenger to tell them the news and to inform them of the day on which *hakika,* a ceremony which takes place on the seventh, ninth, or eleventh day after birth, will be performed. All others are notified by mail. Those to whom a messenger is sent are very close to the family, and they express their joy by giving money—2, 5, or 10 rupees—and a cotton blanket worth from 5 to 10 rupees to the messenger. These relatives come on the designated day, bringing sweets and presents for the mother and the child; they must participate in the joy of the family. Other relatives may also come on the appointed day or at some later date, as it suits them, when they will give presents—clothes for the child and the mother. There are others who will not come, but who will give it some money in the presence of its mother when they see the child for the first time—usually 1, 5, or 10 rupees. This money is called *muñh vekhan,* "to see the face." [12]

When the youngest grandson was born in Bebeji's house in 1945, she sent a messenger to the child's *nanke.* The child's maternal grandmother did not come, but sent one of her sons with 50 rupees for presents. Bebeji refused to take the money. She felt that the *nanke* was not well represented and said: "It is not the money that counts, but it is important to come together and to rejoice on such occasions."

[12] *Muñh vekhan* (but in larger amounts) also is given to the bridegroom or bride by the parents-in-law, when he or she comes to the house for the first time.

XIII

The Rules

The fundamental rule of *vartan bhanji* is reciprocity: a gift should be returned for a gift, a favor should be rendered for a favor, good treatment should be returned for good treatment, and bad treatment or a practical joke in like manner. However, while reciprocity in all dealings is the principal outward manifestation of *vartan bhanji*, what counts most is the attitude of those involved. The material things given are a gauge of a person's character and attitude. Over time, through the numerous dealings, the giving and receiving of gifts, people can appraise one another's ways. Some are very decent in their dealings and give an impression of being genuine and sincere. If they sometimes fail to reciprocate fully in terms of material things, it will not be held against them. They may attend an important event without bringing the gifts they should have brought, yet their very presence and their straightforward explanation of why they are unable to reciprocate is taken as an indication of good will and they are not criticized.

So, for example, when the mother of A.U., a *zamindar* in Dhirke village, died, it was proper to perform *leda*, a ceremony honoring a deceased elderly person who has accomplished his or her life tasks. A.U.'s mother had lived to old age and had discharged her worldly responsibilities, for all her children were married. After a death, the relatives of the deceased come together on the first, on the tenth, and on the thirty-fifth or the fortieth days (depending on who has died). The bereaved family decides on the day *leda* is to take place

—usually the tenth or thirty-fifth day after the death. In this case, the deceased woman had two sons, and their parents-in-law came on the required days and shared in the grief of the family. On the day when *leda* was to be brought, the parents-in-law of one son came but did not bring any gifts. Floods had recently caused considerable damage, especially in the area where their village was situated. The standing crops in their fields and their house were badly damaged. However, they were well represented on the days when their presence was required. The most important people in the household had come, thus indicating how much they honored the dead woman as well as her family. In their previous dealings these people had always been very decent. Consequently, even though the family of the deceased woman did not receive *leda*, they were quite satisfied and felt that the attendance and the explanation given were equal to bringing *leda*.

On the other hand, some people fall far short of their obligations in *vartan bhanji*. They try to cheat the household with whom they are dealing by always accepting the gifts due them on certain occasions and by trying to evade the responsibility of reciprocation on other occasions. In all their dealings they leave the unpleasant impression of deceit as they try to get too much and to give too little. These by their attitude defeat the main purpose of *vartan bhanji*, which is to maintain pleasant relationships.

So, for example, those who deal in *vartan bhanji* with Amaji are never satisfied with her ways. She is the widow of a wealthy *zamindar* of Mohla, and her children and all her relatives call her Amaji, mother. Years ago, at the marriage of J.A., her elder son, the members of the *biraderi* living in the same village sent meals on the days preceding the wedding. A year later, when there was a marriage in the house of one of the *biraderi* from whom Amaji had received a meal at the marriage of J.A., it was her turn to reciprocate. Instead, she left for the city under some pretext and did not fulfill her obligation. A few years later, a son was born to J.A., an occasion for rejoicing when the sisters—actual and in the extended sense of the term—bring gifts but receive more valuable ones from the house in which the child is born. J.A.'s two sisters (actually his father's mother's brother's son's daughter and daughter-in-law) and the mother of one of them brought presents for the infant and its mother, including five frocks for the infant and materials for one outfit for the mother, all of very good quality. In return, Amaji gave three outfits, one for each of the sisters and one for the mother. As these outfits were of inferior quality, the sisters did not accept them. Amaji's family stepped in and tried to convince them that the cloth was of the latest fashion in Lahore, but it was apparent that the materials were gaudy and cheap in quality, so the sisters were not deceived and would not take them. Later Amaji sent the two sisters outfits of a little better quality, but not good enough. One of the pieces was from the outfit they themselves had given to the child's mother (a thing which is often done in this exchange). However, Amaji never sent a third outfit for the mother.

The incident is typical of Amaji's behavior. On occasions for receiving gifts, she emphasizes her relationship to the family which entitles her to receive richly as a daughter of the house; but when it comes to giving, she fails to reciprocate in a proper way. She considers herself wise, but among the people with whom she deals she has earned a reputation of being "clever." When her younger son married, a few of the *biraderis* did not attend the wedding, which cast a bad reflection on her.

However, in general, people are tolerant and do not like to stop dealing in *vartan bhanji*. If one asks why people deal with those who are mean and do not reciprocate properly, the invariable answer is: "It is *vartan bhanji*. Sometimes you get more, sometimes you get less than you have given. In *vartan bhanji* nineteen should equal twenty. One should not be too exacting." It is the general attitude that although the objects which are exchanged are material things and can be measured, so that one knows well how much one has given and how much one has received, what matters most in these dealings is maintaining good relationships.

Even when one of the partners repeatedly fails to behave decently, *vartan bhanji* is not ended abruptly. Instead, people wait for the proper occasion to repay whatever is due, and then balance the account.

This brings us to the second rule of *vartan bhanji*, namely, that while there should be reciprocity, there should never be an equilibrium. The things exchanged should not exactly balance, because this would bring the relationship to an end. In explaining the exchange of gifts, people make an analogy with a pair of scales. They say that the two sides of the scales—or of the relationship—should always be kept vascillating. As a perfect balance brings the needle to a stop, so too, equalization of gifts given and gifts received brings the relationship to a standstill.

So, on the occasion of a marriage, the departing guests receive sweets from the house of marriage. The hostess weighs out the sweets or counts the number of pastries to be given in the presence of the recipient and says to her: "These five *seers* are yours, and these two *seers* are mine." By this the hostess means that previously, on the occasion of a marriage in the household of the recipient, she had received five *seers* of sweets, which she was now returning; to these she added two more *seers* to keep the *vartan bhanji* going. On the next occasion, when she is a recipient, she will receive back her two *seers* plus one, two, or four *seers* more, thus keeping the exchange within a certain range. The amount of sweets given and received by different families varies according to their *vartan bhanji* relationship to the house of marriage.

Or at the marriage of a boy, the father of the groom receives money from the male relatives and friends who are invited to the *meyl*, the gathering one day before *barat*, the wedding party, leaves. This money, called *neondra*, is recorded in the *vehi*, the family register.[1] A man, giving the *neondra*, tells the parent: "There are 20 rupees. Fifteen rupees are yours, and the rest is extra." (The amount given varies from 5 to 101 rupees.) Again, the giver adds a sum to

[1] See Appendix III for a page reproduced from a family register.

the amount owed from a past occasion. The main point is that in order to keep the *vartan bhanji* going, he does not want to balance the account.

Another one of the basic rules of *vartan bhanji* is that no one should go away empty-handed. From the descriptions given of occasions for the giving and receiving of gifts—for instance, at the wedding of a son, when the groom's family gives lavishly to all the daughters of the house, or at the wedding of a daughter, when the bride's family is given lavish presents—it is apparent that on any particular occasion a donor is also (though usually on a quite different scale) a recipient. Analyzing the transactions that take place on some occasion—for instance, the *hakika*, a ceremony performed for a newborn child, to which the guests bring gifts for the family of the infant—it might superficially appear that the exchange of gifts is completed on this very occasion since the guests bring gifts for the family and, before their departure, receive gifts from their hosts.

However, this is not the case. Actually, two different transactions have taken place, each a part of a different cycle. To understand the transactions, one must consider the rule that those who bring a gift should never be sent away without receiving a gift, that is, should not leave empty-handed. So the gift given by the host-recipient was not given in reciprocity for the gift received from the guest-donor. The two acts of giving are components of two different transactions connected only by virtue of having taken place on the same occasion, and these two acts will remain together in the memories of the donors and the recipients. Nevertheless, both transactions will remain incomplete until some big event takes place in the future in the family of a guest-donor involved on this occasion. Then the family which has just received presents will bring its gifts, which should be more or less equivalent to what it has received, thus completing the circuit of the first transaction. Then, the recipients of the gifts on that day will present the family with a departing gift, and so complete the second transaction.

Thus, on one and the same occasion, the two families who are *vartan bhanji* partners are in a double position vis-à-vis each other —both are recipients and both are donors. But giving and receiving on any one occasion are not equivalents. The gift given and the gift received are parts of two separate transactions, each of which can be completed only on some other occasion.[2]

An important rule of *vartan bhanji* is that it should be carried on according to a family's ability to participate in the exchange; since the exchange is always kept in near-balance, this means that the scale of exchange is determined by the ability of the less well-to-do partner. Thus, there are social and economic components in *vartan bhanji*, but these affect primarily those who fall into the second category of persons dealing in gift exchange—those less close to each other. Differences due to social and economic factors do not usually arise between a family and its affinal relatives, for marriages are arranged between families of like economic and social status, but they may occur among the *biraderi*. Among the *biraderi*, some are richer and more influential than others, and some may be quite poor.

A rich *biraderi* has *vartan bhanji* with the poorer ones, but they deal on a small scale. The fact that one family is richer than the other does not mean that it gives valuable gifts and receives less valuable ones in exchange, nor would the poorer relative give a small gift and expect to receive a better one in return. In this connection, the Punjabi say: "*Vartan bhanji* is not charity, nor is it a trade." They say that one can help a poor relative in other ways.

So, for example, at the marriage of S.B., the sister of B.A., who

---

[2] In certain respects, the child's birthday party in the United States provides us with an American parallel to the Punjabi situation and may be used to illustrate the differences between the transactions of giving and receiving that take place on one occasion. When an American child has a birthday party, the guests bring him presents; then usually, in the course of the party, the guests receive favors which they take home. These are not a return for the gifts. Rather, when a guest has a birthday party the host of the previous occasion will bring a present—and also take home a favor.

is one of the poorest among his *biraderi,* two of the well-to-do families of the *biraderi* helped him. They gave a few outfits of good
quality and some bedding for the bride; besides, one family entertained the *barat,* the marriage party, and cooked a meal for at least
a hundred people. This help, however, was not considered to be
vartan bhanji in the usual sense; it was given because the honor of
the *biraderi* was at stake. The *vartan bhanji* here was the relationship existing between the two families.

On the other hand, for a poor relative, *vartan bhanji* is neither a
trade nor a bargain to profit by. So when sweets and clothes are
given to the wedding guests, the poorer *biraderis* receive less sweets
and fewer clothes, of a quality inferior to those given to the rich
relatives with whom *vartan bhanji* is on a larger scale. The point is
that "*vartan bhanji* is not charity." Since it is based on balanced
reciprocity, a rich relative would not give expensive clothes or
quantities of sweets to a poor one, for to do so would be to exert
"pressure," which would cause trouble; equally, the poor relative
would not accept more than he could afford to return.

In this respect, *vartan bhanji* is like a card game in which the
partners agree on the stakes. The stakes may be low or high, but
the game is a game and partners play for the same stakes.

Apart from economic status, social status has considerable bear-
ing on the scale on which a family deals in *vartan bhanji.* A high
social status makes it obligatory for a family to deal on a large scale
with those who are of equal status. Social status means influence,
power, and prestige in the community and may be inherited from
one's ancestors, but the wealth that goes with high social status may
not be there any more. Alternatively, an individual may build up
his social status through personal effort, but may not acquire
enough wealth to support his new position. In the latter case, the
family must deal in *vartan bhanji* in terms of their social rather than
of their economic status.

So, for example, *chowdhri* A.D., in the village of Shadiwal, has
much influence and power but very little land and no money. Never-

theless, he lives on a large scale, and when it comes to dealing in
vartan bhanji with people of an equal social status but richer than
himself, he borrows money so that his family manages to deal on a
scale commensurate with its social status. In this way he has been
able to build up prestige, but to maintain it he must continue to
deal in accordance with his social status.

In contrast, there is N.T., a *zamindar* in Mohla, who has little
land, no influence, and no power. About him the Punjabi would say,
"a starving one who wears white clothes," which is to say that he is
poor but on account of his status does not work on his land. Instead
he rents it and consequently has very little to live on. N.T. has rich
and influential *biraderis* in the neighboring city, whom he often
visits and with whom he carries on *vartan bhanji* on a scale he can
afford. He is treated with respect and feels in no way inferior to his
rich relatives. He feels that they are all equal in their inherited
status, for they have an immediate ancestor in common, and whatever some of them have recently gained in money, prestige, and
power does not concern him. He is in no way obligated to them;
whatever he receives in *vartan bhanji,* he returns in the same way.
When he is in need of money, as was the case when his children
married, he borrows from people other than his rich *biraderis.* In
exchanging gifts, he may deal on a very low scale, but when it
comes to treatment, he demands respect and consideration commensurate with his inherited high social status. In this case, N.T.
deals in *vartan bhanji* in terms of his economic status, but this does
not affect his inherited social status.

The manner in which *vartan bhanji* is carried out is also affected
in many subtle ways by the attitudes of the two families who are
partners. On certain occasions a family invites relatives and close
friends to attend a ceremony at its home. During their visit the
guests should be treated to good meals, they should be given good
sleeping accommodations, and their servants should also be well
treated. Still, it may happen that certain guests feel that they have
not been properly entertained—they were not served on time or

were not treated in the manner to which close kin are entitled, or their servants were neglected. On the other hand, sometimes the hosts may feel hurt if the invited family is not well represented, that is, if it did not send to the ceremony its most important members, and thus did not show enough respect and did not give enough significance to the occasion. In such cases, the contact between the two families does not promote any warmth of feeling and, although they may exchange gifts and continue their *vartan bhanji*, the chances are that in the long run their relationship will dwindle away.

As related families meet on many different occasions, their mutual attitudes and behavior will determine whether the *vartan bhanji* relationship will be a very pleasant and wholehearted affair or merely a nominal one. We may take as examples of two such contrasting relationships the interactions of three families we shall designate as Family A (Amaji), Family B (Bebeji), and Family C (Phuphi).[3]

Family A and Family B are *biraderi;* that is, the husbands belong to the same patrilineage. The wife in Family C is the daughter of Family B.

According to custom, the daughter has a right in her father's house. It is her right to visit her paternal home regularly during the year and to receive presents. Every visit brings the two families— Family B, Phuphi's brother's family (for, her father being dead, her brother is now the head of her paternal home), and Family C, her family by marriage—into closer contact. If her brother's wife in Family B receives her well and makes her stay pleasant and sends her off with good presents and many sweets, and if, on the whole, throughout her visit the atmosphere is agreeable and friendly, then the relationship will become closer. Phuphi—father's sister, as she is called in Family B—will bring her children with her and strong bonds will develop between the two families.

---

[3] The names of the women at the head of these households are given in parenthesis.

In turn every event in Phuphi's house, the home of Family C, will be duly attended by the people from her brother's house, and if they too are properly entertained and are given appropriate presents, and if even the *kammis* who have accompanied them are well tipped and are given choice food and gifts of clothes, then this pleasant relationship will bring the two families still closer together. The mutually pleasing attitudes of Family B and Family C make for "good *vartan bhanji.*"

Once established, a good relationship between a family and the married daughter's parents-in-law can last for two generations or, at most, for three. But when a very warm relationship has been established, the two families will arrange another marriage and so create a new link to keep the relationship alive. Thus within four generations four girls from Family B have married into Family C, and six girls from Family C into Family B.[4]

In contrast, let us examine the relationship between Family A and Family B. The men of these two households are the sons of parallel cousins and belong to the same *biraderi*. As both families have had a number of sons and daughters, there have been enough ceremonies to attend in each and gifts to be exchanged between them. In Family A, there have been in this generation at least five births, two circumcisions, and five marriages. In Family B there have also been births, circumcisions, and marriages. The two families attended each other's celebrations and exchanged gifts. But somehow the relationship remained perfunctory. The difficulty is that one side—Family A—seemed not to deal properly in *vartan bhanji* as Amaji received much but tried to get away with giving as little as possible, and Family A failed to show much consideration for Family B. As a result, although there have been marriageable children in both families, there have been no intermarriages in these two families in this generation. Except for meeting on the major occasions when all the relatives should come together, neither family

[4] See Appendix IV, in which a diagram is given showing the intermarriages in three families, including Families B and C here described.

has shown any desire to elaborate the relationship through more contacts than have been absolutely necessary to maintain minimal *vartan bhanji.*

The proper display of articles given and received is an important part of correct behavior in *vartan bhanji.* The person, usually a woman, who brings a gift presents it to the person in charge of the household of the recipient, usually a woman, very soon after arriving. Everything that is brought is neatly put together. If cloth for *jowṛas* is brought, the donor shows each outfit of three pieces and tells for whom it is intended; if sweets are brought, they are weighed or counted and the quality is noted. Similarly the quality of the material for the outfits is taken into account. For some of the outfits the three pieces of cloth match, which shows that they were carefully selected, but others are put together just to complete the outfit. As the pieces are of standard length, and usually of a current fashion, women who are well versed in the quality of materials can immediately appraise the value.

The recipient of a gift is not expected to thank the giver. But each present is displayed to all the members of the family and to the guests and to the people of the village who may come to the house.

The gifts presented to the guests by the hosts are given just at the time of departure. A daughter-in-law of a house or an older woman of the household gives them to the guests and, if cloth is given, says for whom each outfit is intended. Sweets are weighed or counted in the presence of the recipient.

The proper thing for a woman to do in going to a wedding is to show to all the people of her village with whom she deals in *vartan bhanji* all the gifts she is taking to the celebration. When she returns, she will describe the marriage to the same people, including all the transactions which took place, so that the visitors will feel that they have participated in it. She will mention how she and her family were treated, and will show the gifts and distribute the sweets received at the ceremony.

By so doing, a woman who has participated in some big event indicates that everything went off well. But it has another significance also. The visiting women who are her audience before and afterward weigh in their minds all the details of what has taken place, take note of what was brought, and form a clear opinion about how the person who attended the ceremony stands among her relatives, which in turn reflects upon her way of dealing in *vartan bhanji*.

Of a person who goes to a celebration without showing the gifts she is taking and without showing what she has received or distributing the sweets, people in the village say: "She stole away like a thief and came home like a thief."

Dealing in *vartan bhanji* is a source of prestige to all those concerned in the transactions; hence proper behavior involves the full display of gifts at every stage in the exchange so that there may be the largest possible audience of appreciative critics of things well done.

XIV

Establishing Relationships

In order to enter into *vartan bhanji* relations, one must have an independent household. *Vartan bhanji* provides an introduction to adult social life and is the means of establishing and broadening a family's social contacts. Actually, one inherits these relationships in the same way that one inherits property or *seyp* relationships, but the man who sets up a separate household may either increase or decrease the circle of families with whom he wishes to deal in *vartan bhanji*. To deal with many people takes much time and money, for one must attend the ceremonies at which gift exchanges take place, yet in terms of having many established contacts, of being close to one's relatives, and of having many good friends, it is rewarding. The extensiveness of one's *vartan bhanji* relationships is an indication of one's social status, prestige, influence, and ability to deal properly with people.

As long as the married sons live with their parents, their mother is the main representative of the household; she deals in *vartan bhanji* with her husband's relatives, with her own relatives, and, as the sons and daughters marry, with the children's parents-in-law and their relatives. After the sons have established their separate households, the main *ghar* continues with its circle of *vartan bhanji*, but from this time on, each son takes initial steps in establishing his own circle.

This will be done gradually, for contact with the parental home is constantly kept up, but as relatives and friends come to visit the parents, the sons and their wives help to entertain the guests and invite them to a meal in their own house, thus indicating that they have separate households. It will gradually become known that the son of a certain family has a separate household. Then on some special occasion such as the birth of a child, it will be appropriate to start *vartan bhanji.*

So, for example, G.D., the second son of a *chowdhri* in Gudyala village, was preparing to celebrate the *hakika* of his fifth child. *Hakika* is a ceremony performed on the seventh, ninth, or eleventh day after the birth of a child, but it is especially celebrated for a firstborn son or a child born in a family which has had no children for years. In the case of G.D., it was the fifth child, and had he been living in his father's house, the *hakika* would not have been celebrated. But now, since he had a separate household, this was an appropriate occasion to start *vartan bhanji.* So he invited the relatives and friends who, knowing that he had a separate household, understood that this was an invitation to start *vartan bhanji;* not to have attended the celebration would have amounted to a refusal to do so.

One of the families he invited was his *nanke,* the household of his maternal relatives in Mohla, which now included the widow of his maternal uncle, her widowed daughter-in-law, a widowed daughter, an unmarried son, an unmarried daughter, and grandchildren. The relatives from Mohla were represented by the daughter-in-law, a widowed daughter, an adult son, and two grandchildren. The head of the household could not come, but she sent her daughter-in-law who, being the widow of a much-loved eldest son, was much respected among the relatives. On these occasions, each family should be well represented, yet should not send too many people because this would put "pressure" on the host.

These guests from Mohla brought a few outfits for the newborn, a silk outfit for the mother and silk outfits for the infant's older siblings. The presents were delivered soon after the arrival to the wife of G.D.'s youngest brother, who was entertaining the guests and was in charge of the household. In addition to the clothes brought as gifts, when the guests saw the newborn for the first time, the woman representing the family from Mohla gave the child 10 rupees, as *muñh vekhan*, "seeing the face"—a sign of welcome to the child. This money is given in the presence of the child's mother and other adults, who will remember the amount and by whom it was given.

The visitors from Mohla were very well entertained during their two-day stay, and just before their departure the wife of the youngest brother brought the gifts presented by the household of G.D. and gave them to the daughter-in-law from Mohla. There were silk outfits for the two women who had come to visit and for the two children, and the *kammi* who had accompanied them was given a very good tip. *Vartan bhanji* relationship was thus started between G.D. and his relatives from Mohla and also with other relatives who attended the *hakika* ceremony.

On the day of the *hakika*, besides the members of the *biraderi* who live in the same village and the relatives who came from other villages, *kammi* women and the wives of other *zamindars* in the village came bringing sweets, or sweets and money for the child. They also brought a certain amount of wheat (two to four *seers*) for the barber who prepared the feast; if some *kammi* had assisted the barber, the two would have shared the wheat.

The people who bring wheat and sweets and money in this way have *vartan bhanji* with the family; the scale of the exchange varies depending upon what a family can afford and how close it feels to the recipient's family. A well-to-do *kammi* who has been attached for years to a *zamindar's* family may deal on the same scale as a child of the *zamindar's* family.

After the *hakika* ceremony it may happen that there will be another important ceremony in the same household. The people with whom G.D.'s family has now established *vartan bhanji* relationships again will be invited and will bring gifts, and when they depart may receive gifts of clothes, or gifts of clothes and sweets, or only sweets, in accordance with the demands of the occasion. In this way, the family of G.D. will have been the recipients on two successive occasions, but there is time enough for them to reciprocate because *vartan bhanji* is a long-term relationship in which there are many occasions on which to complete transactions and to start a new series.

Although the new household initially establishes *vartan bhanji* with the same people with whom the parents have dealt, from generation to generation the circle of people changes. With the passage of time, the mother of the older generation may have almost completed the dealings with some relatives who have moved far away or with whom common interests have decreased; the sons may not deal with these. On the other hand, the relationship may be intensified with a different set of relatives, and new friends may be added as well. Then, too, each man deals with the relatives of his wife and with his siblings' parents-in-law and their relatives.

XV

Women's Role and Men's Role

Women play the more active role in *vartan bhanji*. They represent
the family at all the ceremonies, for one's presence on these occasions is as important as the giving and receiving of presents. They
conduct most of the transactions. And they are the guardians of
vartan bhanji, who know to whom and when and how much a family
is to give as well as from whom and when and how much it should
receive. Every detail of past, present, and even future transactions
is as clear and simple to women as are the most familiar possessions
in their households, of which they are able to give an account at
any moment. But men also, on certain occasions, take an active part
in *vartan bhanji* transactions. It is not easy to make a simple differ-
entiation between the types of transactions in which men and
women, respectively, are actively involved, but it can be said that,
in general, where men are involved the transaction is one that goes
outside the home—for instance, where *vartan bhanji* is between two
villages. Also, with a few exceptions, where the exchange of material things is concerned, men are mainly involved with money.
(Women also give and receive money, but men do not usually give
other types of presents, though they receive them.)

To deal well in *vartan bhanji* it is necessary to know well all the
complex rules. It is always the oldest woman of a household who is
in full command of the essential information. She remembers everything that has been given away or received during her lifetime—
and sometimes even before that. Every time an exchange of gifts

takes place, after the guests have left, the old grandmother is sure to enumerate all the transactions that have taken place between her household and that of each relative and friend who was present. The quality of the yard goods received, the people to whom they were given, the amount of money, the amount and quality of the sweets received—all will be mentioned. The generosity and outgoing nature of the partner will be praised, and if a partner has been niggardly that will not be overlooked either.

On one occasion, a *zamindar* woman in Mohla was telling a group of women how well she had celebrated the marriage of her son and described to them the superior quality of the *ledus*—a kind of pastry—she had distributed in the village. Thereupon Zaynab Bibi, an old *musalliñ*, that is, a woman of the caste of agricultural laborers, brought out a small, dried-out *ledu* which she had carefully preserved for twelve years and, displaying it before the boasting *zamindar* woman, asked with scorn: "Is this not the *ledu* which you distributed at the marriage of your son?" This *ledu* Zaynab Bibi had preserved for years because it was of inferior quality, and she had waited for an opportunity to expose a *zamindar* woman who was always boasting. Although Zaynab Bibi was a *musalliñ*, she commanded much respect in the village for her knowledge and ability to deal properly in *vartan bhanji*. At the marriage of her own sons the food and the *ledus* she distributed in the village were of superior quality, so she was justifiably proud.

This act of Zaynab Bibi was typical, for in every village there are a few old women who are the authorities on and, therefore, know, so to speak, all the laws of *vartan bhanji*. Should anyone try to evade any of the customary requirements, these women would raise their voices and openly criticize them. If a person does not perform the customary distributions in a way appropriate to his status and tries to excuse himself on grounds of ignorance, nobody accepts this. People say: "If you did not know what or how much or to whom to give, there are enough people who know and whom you could have consulted."

From her childhood a girl acquires the habit of keeping tally of all the things given away or received by the family on special occasions and also during first visits to relatives. She has, for example, seen her paternal grandmother collect *ghi* for making sweets to be distributed and store rolls of white broadcloth, silk, chiffon, material for men's clothing, and fine muslin for turbans to be given away as outfits for the daughters of the house and for the sons-in-law at the wedding of her elder brother and her young paternal aunt.

The use of a yardstick, of scales, and of standard measures for wheat and rice is very common in the household in connection with giving and receiving gifts. As she grows up, the young girl becomes proficient in handling the yardstick to measure off the cloth for an outfit to be given away, in weighing the sweets received or given, and she is able to tell at a glance the exact amount of wheat, corn, or millet brought as *veyl*, a gift brought on special occasions by the village people who have *vartan bhanji* with a family.

The young wife hears her mother-in-law repeatedly describe the gift exchanges of her husband's family with its circle of relatives and friends and also with her own (the young wife's) family. She accompanies her mother-in-law on many occasions and receives outfits as the daughter-in-law of that family. Gradually she herself starts dealing in *vartan bhanji* with her married sisters and female cousins. By the time her mother-in-law dies, she has taken over the management of the house and has become well equipped to carry on the dealings handed down by her parents-in-law and those she herself has started.

In the course of her training she has also learned how to refuse a gift. On some occasion, for instance, when a son is born to her father's cousin's son, she presents a gift and receives an outfit. But if she thinks the outfit is not as good as it should be, she rejects it scornfully. On another occasion she may refuse a gift for other reasons. At some ceremony, the donor may include her by extension of the meaning of the term "father's sister" in that category of aunts and may present her with an outfit. But she may consider it wiser not to accept it because the status conferred on her may in the future put her under an obligation which she may not care to fulfill.

While women take part in *vartan bhanji* transactions on all occasions, the transactions involving actual gift exchange in which men take part are limited in number and take place only on a few important occasions. Among these transactions are the giving and receiving of *roti*, literally bread or food but in this case the money collected at the ceremony on the death of an old person, and also the giving and receiving of the *neondra*, the money given to the bridegroom's parents by the wedding guests. At a marriage, men of the bridegroom's family also give *thehan*, a copper plate, sweets, and money, to the married daughters of the bridegroom's village living in the village of the bride; they give *ratha chari*, gifts of money to the bards gathered in the bride's village from other villages whose daughters and daughters' daughters are married into the bridegroom's village; they give *chul*, literally hearth but in this case money given to the households of *kammis* living in the bride's village; and the male wedding guests give *veyl*, small sums of money, to the bards who entertain the guests at a wedding, who then sing songs praising the donor's village and the village where the marriage is taking place.

There are also certain individual gifts which are made by a man. So, for instance, at a wedding the mother's brother (or the mother's brother's son) gives *khara lhai*, a valuable present given when the bride or bridegroom takes a ritual bath. And the bridegroom gives his sisters, female cousins, and so on, *vag pharai*, literally holding the reins but here money to free his horse so he may leave with the *barat*, the wedding party, to fetch the bride.

But for the most part, the exchange of clothes, food, sweets, and the money given at times of sickness, as *selami*, and on other occasions—all these transactions are the sole responsibility of women.

The presents which a true daughter receives from her parents (or later from her brother as the representative of her parental home) are phrased as "the daughter's right in her father's house," so that, ultimately, the source of the presents is the man. But the transactions themselves, with the daughter as her right and with others in *vartan bhanji,* are regarded as chiefly the responsibility of the women.

Both men and women have an undisputed recognition and respect for each other's parts in *vartan bhanji.* Visiting on various occasions takes time and money for the trips, causes inconveniences, and often disrupts the schooling of the younger children. Yet all the difficulties are borne willingly and a woman is never prevented from carrying out these important activities. Her knowledge of how things should be done and her ability to do them well add to the status and increase the *izzet* of the whole family.

XVI

At a Marriage

Although gift exchange is an important aspect of all big occasions when people come together, it reaches a climax in the ceremonies connected with marriage. For this is the occasion when the relationships established by a household with its *biraderi,* affinal kin, friends, *seypis,* with the *zamindars* and the *kammis* of the village and of neighboring villages all come into play. For this reason, marriage provides the best illustration of what is involved in all the different kinds of distributions. Therefore the description which follows of the types of articles used in *vartan bhanji* will focus upon a wedding.

The celebration of marriage consists of a number of events which stretch out over several months. It begins with the *gala,* the ceremony at which the opening of marriage ceremonies is officially announced, and ends with the *tarwianda,* the third visit of the bride to the household of her parents-in-law.[1]

The principal gifts involved in *vartan bhanji* are sweets, uncooked and cooked foods, yard goods for clothes, and money. Each of these is dealt with in turn.

SWEETS

On all the occasions when gift exchanges take place, sweets are very important. There are different varieties of sweets: *ledu,*[2]

[1] See Appendix V, Ceremonies Connected with Marriage, for a chart showing the sequence of ceremonies in the boy's and in the girl's home.
[2] *Ledu* is a pastry made of dough with a filling of almonds, coconut, raisins,

mithyai, bundi, kachi, pini,[3] *panjiri,*[4] *ptassa,*[5] *gur,*[6] and *bid,*[7] which are given or received according to the occasion.

A young couple may be engaged for a period of a few months to a year, during which the girl's family must prepare the dowry and everything needed to meet the expenses of the marriage. Since the boy's family has less to do, it waits for the girl's family to make the first move. When the girl's side is nearly ready, the parents of the couple get together and set the date of the *barat,* the party of men who come to fetch the bride, which includes the bridegroom, his close relatives, *biraderi,* and friends. For the boy's side, the day of *barat* is when the party of men leaves the bridegroom's village; for the girl's side it is the day the men arrive in her village.

sugar, and fried cream of wheat. The whole pastry is fried in *ghi.* It varies in size, from one-eighth to half a *seer,* and in quality, depending on the filling and the amount of *ghi* used; the poor fry it in vegetable oil. When *ledus* are given or received in any quantity, the number of pieces are counted and the quality and size are well remembered.

[3] *Mithyai, bundi,* and *kachi pini* are pastries all of which contain coconut, almonds, sugar, and *ghi* but vary in the admixture of fine wheat flour, gram, or rice flour. The quality depends on the amount of *ghi* used and on the proportion of coconut and almonds. When given in quantity, they are weighed and the quality is noted. These are usually given together; for convenience, I shall henceforth refer to them as "assorted sweets."

[4] *Panjiri* is a mixture of cream of wheat and of white (refined) or brown sugar fried in *ghi.* The quality depends on the amount of *ghi* used, and white sugar is considered to be superior to the local brown sugar. A married woman usually brings *panjiri* whenever she comes back from a visit to her parental home and sometimes when she goes to visit her parents. A new bride would seldom bring *panjiri* on one of her three initial visits, and it is more common for a poor *zamindar* or a *kammi* woman to bring *panjiri* than for a rich one. However, if the women are in a hurry, even a rich *zamindar* may give her daughter *panjiri* to take to her parents-in-law, for of all sweets it can be prepared quickly and with the least trouble; in this case plenty of *ghi* is used and raisins and almonds added. The amount brought by a woman would vary from two to five *seers.* This is distributed in the village, a plateful to each household.

[5] *Ptassa* is a sugar candy which is very light in weight. It can be bought in the market and can be kept for months. When it is distributed, a handful is given to each person.

[6] *Gur* is brown sugar. When it is distributed, it is given in lumps varying in size from one quarter to one *seer.*

[7] *Bid* is a mixture of dried coconut, raisins, dates, and almonds. Together with the mixed fruit, henna leaves are also brought as an important part of *bid;* the henna—used as a cosmetic—may be as much as two and a half *seers.*

The family of a boy or a girl in inviting guests to a marriage mails letters to relatives and friends who live far away and to those who are not considered very important. To important relatives who live within fifty miles, they send a messenger. This man, usually a barber or some other *kammi* of the house, delivers the message orally and also brings the household *ptassa,* sugar candy, the amount of which varies from a handful to one or even two and a half *seers.* The messenger is given a gift of money at each household.

Once the date of the *barat* has been fixed, the two families perform the *gala* ceremony, announcing the opening of the cycle of marriage ceremonies, each in its own village. *Gala* may take place three or four weeks before the *barat;* in the interval each family has its own schedule of events. At the *gala* all the women of the village—and from the outside only the married daughters, that is, the sisters and paternal aunts of the bride or bridegroom—are invited to the house of marriage, and on that day the families of the bride and bridegroom each distribute *gur* in its own village. At the marriage of her older son, the mother of the *chowdhri* of Mohla distributed three *maunds* of *gur* (one *maund* equals 82 pounds).

After the *gala,* the period of intensive preparation begins in the boy's house as well as in the girl's. Among the *kammis* of the house, each one has his special work to do. The carpenter and the *musalli* have to collect fuel, for much of it is needed. Before starting his work, the carpenter comes to the house of marriage and informs the woman at the head of the household that he is ready to begin. Thereupon she gives him a big lump of *gur* (about one *seer*). This is to start his work with pleasantness and sweetness. The tailor before cutting cloth to make outfits for the bride or other members of the house of marriage is also given *gur.* A *kammi* is sent to other villages to buy the large quantities of *ghi* needed for cooking food and sweets. At a wedding of a well-to-do *zamindar* from one hundred fifty to two hundred *seers* of *ghi* are used. The women *kammis* help to clean the wheat. The potter takes the wheat to the mill. The barber goes to the city to rent a number of huge cauldrons for cooking, to sample rice, to buy quantities of spices, and to engage a few barbers to help him in cooking. Before starting any work, every *kammi* is given his share of *gur*. The work is usually started on an auspicious day—Monday, Wednesday, or Saturday.

A week before the *barat*, a professional sweetmaker from the city is hired to cook the sweets. People do not like to buy sweets at the market because they want to be sure that their sweets are made of pure *ghi* and good ingredients. The sweetmaker prepares hundreds of pounds of assorted sweets and hundreds of *ledus*. These are stored in huge tin boxes. The families of both the girl and the boy prepare a great quantity of sweets. At a wedding on a smaller scale, the sweets are prepared by the barber's wife, assisted by the women of the household.

In the boy's village, a day or two before the departure of the *barat*, the bridegroom's household distributes *ledus* in the village. At the marriage of her elder son, the mother of the *chowdhri* of Mohla distributed 1,000 *ledus*, each weighing a quarter *seer*. Every household in the village received a portion, the number depending upon the number of people in it, including the married daughters and father's sisters. Each person received more than one *ledu*. Seventeen years have passed, but people in Mohla still remember these *ledus*, their number, and quality.

At the girl's house, a few days before the *barat*, the bride's married sisters, her *phuphi* (father's sister), and her *nanke* (mother's mother, mother's brothers and their wives, and mother's married sisters) arrive bringing clothes for her and sweets. Each of them brings 101 *ledus*.

In the boy's house, his married sisters and his *phuphi* arrive bringing him an outfit and a gold ring. Each also brings 5, 7, 11, or 15 *seers* of assorted sweets.

At the bridegroom's house, as soon as the *barat* has left for the bride's village, the *meylis*, the wedding guests, are ready to go home. Before leaving they receive from the bridegroom's family clothes and sweets. Each family is given a few *ledus*—10 to 30 pieces—and assorted sweets. The *nanke*—the household of the mother's mother of the groom—gets 15 to 21 *seers* because it is the marriage of their daughter's son.

Though the guests leave, the married sisters and the *phuphi* of the bridegroom remain. They will wait for the bride to come on her first and second visits before they leave. Before going away, each will receive, besides other valuable gifts, plenty of sweets, both *ledus* and assorted sweets.

In the bride's house, after the bride has left with the *barat*, the wedding guests are ready to go. Before departing, each of the families receives *ledus,* assorted sweets, and some of the *bid*, brought by the bridegroom together with *varasui*, the presents of clothes and ornaments given the bride by the parents-in-law.

The guests—those who have attended the celebration at either the girl's or the boy's family—take the sweets back to their villages. There they send a little to each of the households of their intimate friends, relatives, and the *kammis* with whom they have close *vartan bhanji* relations. These sweets are sent as a token to show that "they were welcomed at the ceremony which they attended" and that "everything went off smoothly."

The bride comes to her husband's village bringing *ledus*, which are distributed in the village. People will well remember the quality of the *ledus* brought by the bride.

On the following day, someone from the bride's family comes to fetch the bride and the bridegroom. The person who comes brings 15 to 21 *seers* of sweets, most of which are distributed in the boy's village.

The couple goes back to visit the bride's family; this is the bridegroom's *muklawa*. The bridegroom's mother does not send any sweets with them. After the couple has stayed in the girl's village for two or three days, the bridegroom's parents, or some close relative, come to fetch them and bring from 15 to 21 *seers* of sweets of a different kind from those brought from the bride's house. Most of these sweets are distributed in the girl's village.

Now the bride goes on her second visit, *muklawa,* to her parents-in-law. Her mother sends along 101 *ledus* or 21 *seers* of assorted sweets, a portion of which is distributed in the boy's village. At this time the sisters and the *phuphi* of the groom go home to their villages, taking with them their gifts and sweets.

Then someone comes from the bride's family to fetch her home. He brings along sweets which are distributed in the bridegroom's village. The bride goes back to her *peke,* with or without the bridegroom, and takes with her sweets from her mother-in-law, which are distributed in her own village.

When the bride has visited her own home for a few weeks, the bridegroom or someone from his family comes to fetch her and brings along sweets or fruit, which are distributed in her village. When the bride goes on her third visit, the *tarwianda,* to her husband's family, she takes along 101 *ledus,* which are distributed in her husband's village. With this distribution the giving of sweets in connection with the marriage festivities comes to an end.

FOOD

Food, both cooked and uncooked, is important on all the major occasions, and has its particular place in *vartan bhanji.* During marriage celebrations there are two distinct currents in the flow of food. The main current goes out of the house of marriage and a subsidiary one comes in—the latter a mere trickle compared to the former.

Immediately after the *gala* ceremony—in both homes—the *kammis* of the house and some other *kammis* get busy with preparations. From that day on, they eat their meals at the house of marriage or take the cooked meal home. This continues for a month until the wedding day, and during this period food is cooked in great abundance.

At the *maiyañ,* the ceremony of tying a bracelet of knotted colored thread around the wrists of the bride and the bridegroom, the house of marriage distributes boiled wheat in the village. The amount distributed varies from ten to two hundred *seers.*

During the week preceding the *barat,* the families of the bride and of the bridegroom perform the ceremonies of *var* and *sambhal* by distributing uncooked and cooked food in their respective villages. According to their means, at the *var* they may distribute wheat and lentils, or wheat and meat (which is a step higher). The meat may be either mutton or beef (mutton being preferred as superior to beef). Sometimes, in addition to food, money is given. At the *sambhal,* a plateful of cooked rice is sent to each household in the village.

This food is distributed to the village at large because, essentially, every family has *vartan bhanji* with every other family in the village. Some households can never reciprocate, yet by leaving no one out and thus by having some relationship with everyone, this is a step in maintaining *vartan bhanji.*

The house of marriage also receives food on several occasions. On the day of the *gala,* wheat is brought by the women who attend the ceremony. With the exception of the very poor *kammis* and a very few *zamindar* women, who are on that level of *vartan bhanji* with the family that they come and congratulate them but do not exchange anything (for *vartan bhanji* is not limited to material things alone), all the women bring vessels filled with wheat in amounts varying from two to four *seers.* This wheat is called *veyl.* It is poured into one pile, and may amount to as much as one *maund.* This is for the *kammis* of the house; the barber's wife and the *musalli* woman who work for the family divide the grain between them.

At the *maiyañ,* the women of the village who have *vartan bhanji* with the house of marriage again bring wheat to be divided among the *kammis* of the house. On the day of *maiyañ* and on the following days, the house of marriage also receives cooked food from the houses of their *biraderis* with whom they have *vartan bhanji* and for whom they have cooked food on similar occasions. The food sent by the *biraderis* is the main meal of the day—the evening meal. It is sent in double the amount needed to feed the household and all the *kammis* who work for them, so the family feels free to send the extra food to households in the village with whom they are on the level of *vartan bhanji* to exchange food.

Two days before the *barat,* the household of marriage receives uncooked food from those people in the village and in the neighboring villages to whom they have previously sent uncooked food on similar occasions. This may be sent in any one of the following combinations: rice, *ghi,* and refined sugar; *seviyañ* (vermicelli), *ghi,* and refined sugar; or rice, *ghi,* and *guṛ* (brown sugar). The amounts vary. Of wheat, at least four *seers* and at most eight *seers* are sent; of sugar, one *seer;* of ghi, at least half a *seer* and at most two *seers.*

On the days of the *meyl,* immediately preceding the *barat,* when all the *meylis,* the wedding guests, have arrived, huge cauldrons of food are cooked. Then the house of the bridegroom sends full trays of cooked food—*pilau* (salted rice), a meat dish, sweet rice, and bread—to the families in its own and in neighboring villages who are on the same level of *vartan bhanji,* that is, who have previously sent cooked food on similar occasions.

In the boy's house, when food is served on the days of the *meyl,* the order of serving is as follows: first, the men *meylis* eat; second (or simultaneously), the women *meylis,* the children, and the women of the house eat in the women's section of the house; at the same time, the trays of food are sent to the families with whom the family have *vartan bhanji;* third, all the *biraderis* who live in the same village and who have been helping and also the men of the house; fourth, the *kammis* who have worked throughout the previous month, other *kammis* of the same village who have been helping out, and also *kammis* who have come from neighboring villages; and fifth, the *mirasis* (village bards), who always know about marriages, and also the poor and the beggars—whoever comes along.

Meanwhile, at the girl's house, the *meylis* gather at least two days before the arrival of the *barat*. There, too, great quantities of food are cooked, for there may be anywhere from 30 to 150 guests, besides the *kammis*. The choicest meal is cooked and served to the *barat* upon their arrival. At this meal the *baratis* are served separately, as a group, and they eat first. Then the *meylis* are served, and after them the rest of the people in the same order as at the boy's house.

At the marriage of the sister of A.M., a moderately well-to-do *zamindar* in Mohla, over 700 people were fed on the evening when the *barat* arrived in the village, and late at night the voice of the night watchman could be heard as he passed by shouting: "Is there anybody left who has not eaten? Any passerby, anyone is welcome to eat!"

Whenever there is a marriage, all the neighboring villages are half deserted, for most of the *kammis* go to the feast to eat and to bring home full trays of rice and meat. The *musallis* also bring back pieces of bread and leftovers from the plates for their animals. No person is given leftover food to eat, because that is a sin.

When the bridegroom comes home bringing the bride with him, his family cooks *khichṛi*, rice with lentils, and distributes it in the village. Then when the bride returns to her home on the following day with the bridegroom for his *muklawa*, the *biraderis* of the bride's family, who are on *vartan bhanji* with them, invite the newly wed couple and the members of the girl's household to a meal.

At the marriage of R.B., the younger sister of the *chowdhri* of Mohla, when the bride and bridegroom returned to the village, three houses of *biraderis* invited them to a meal. As time was short, they accepted two invitations to meals, and the third household invited them to afternoon tea.

When the young couple returns to the bridegroom's village for the bride's *muklawa*, the *biraderis* of the bridegroom's family invite them and also the members of the boy's household to a meal as part of their *vartan bhanji*.

And when, finally, the bride comes for her *tarwianda*, the third visit to her parents-in-law, her mother-in-law asks her to cook *khichri*, rice with lentils, which is distributed in the village. Cooking *khichri* is a signal to the bride to take up her household duties in the house of her parents-in-law. With this, the distributions of food in connection with the marriage festivities come to an end.

CLOTH

The exchange and distribution of sweets and of food are *vartan bhanji* in its preliminary stages. This dealing in sweets and, particularly, in food is carried on with an extensive group of relatives, friends, *kammis* who work for the family, neighbors, people in the village and in neighboring villages. However, when it comes to dealing in cloth and money, the group is the restricted circle of one's close *biraderis*, affinal relatives, and very close friends. As with sweets and food, the widest distributions of cloth and of money take place during the various stages of the marriage ceremonies. And, as in the case of sweets and food, those who celebrate the event give away a great number of *jowras*, native outfits of clothing, and receive only a few.[8]

---

[8] All the *jowras* which are given consist of three unsewn pieces of cloth. The *jowra* for a woman consists of the *dupata*, headcloth (2½ yards), the *shelwar*, baggy pants (4 to 4½ yards) or, for an old woman, a piece of cloth (4½ yards) or a ready made but unsewn piece for a *lungi*, wrap-around; and the *kamiz*, tunic (2½ to 3½ yards). The length of this piece varies, as the *kamiz* may be worn long or short, according to fashion. The pieces given should be always of new, fresh cloth bought for the occasion. Women know the current prints on the market and which yard goods are fashionable, and they can tell at a glance or by touching the cloth within what price range it belongs. The well-to-do give away outfits of silk with chiffon head covers, but there are different qualities of silk and chiffon. The best ones go to those with whom one is on close terms and with whom one has much *vartan bhanji* and exchanges things of the best quality. To poor relatives one gives *jowras* of inferior quality, for otherwise, as the Punjabi say, "there is too much pressure" on them. The poor *kammis* give *jowras* of cheap artificial silk with thin head covers. From 1950 to 1955, the cost of an average silk *jowra* was from 50 to 100 rupees (3.3 rupees then equaled one dollar); a *jowra* of cheap artificial silk then cost between 12 and 15 rupees.

A *jowra* given to a man consists usually of only two lengths of yard goods, for the *shelwar* (4 to 4½ yards) and for a shirt, which is worn long (3½ yards). For *shelwars* broadcloth is given; there are only a few standard qualities. For

But before the ceremonies connected with marriage begin, the mother of the bride—as also the mother of the groom—receives a *jowṛa* for herself from her *peke*, her paternal family. If the woman's mother is living, she brings it; if she is not, then it is brought by the woman's older brother's wife. Or, if there is no one to bring it from the *peke*, her husband's sister, the *phuphi* of the house, will give it. This *jowṛa* is called *hath phareda*, meaning to plunge one's hands (into marriage). Receiving this outfit signifies that the mother can now launch the wedding festivities.

At the marriage of Phuphi's (father's sister of the *chowdhri* of Mohla) son's son, F.B. (the mother of the bridegroom) had no one to give her *hath phareda*. F.B.'s mother was not living, and although she had brothers, she had neither maintained good relations with her brothers' wives nor participated in their important events; they, in their turn, never gave her the presents which a daughter has a right to receive from her father's house, nor did they come on any occasion of hers. So she received none of the things given at a wedding by the *peke*. Then Bebeji (mother of the *chowdhri* of Mohla, who is Phuphi's brother's wife) came to the rescue. She patted F.B. on the back and said: "Don't you worry, I will make you my daughter and give you *hath phareda*."

On this same occasion, Bebeji gave another *hath phareda* to

---

shirts, striped mercerized cotton—poplin—is usually given, but the best material is a plain white Chinese silk with the trade mark of "two horses." Sometimes muslin for the *pagṛi*, turban, is added (5¼ yards). A *jowṛa* of good quality for a man costs between 35 and 45 rupees and the *pagṛi* costs an additional 15 rupees. A *jowṛa* for a man given by a poor *kammi* costs between 10 and 15 rupees.

Children are also given *jowṛas*, the length of the pieces of cloth depending on their age. Girls below five and infants are given an unsewn piece of cloth large enough for a frock.

One of the main preparations for a marriage is the buying of the cloth for the *jowṛas*. The house of marriage buys many rolls of white broadcloth of different grades, rolls of cloth of varying quality for shirts, rolls of muslin for turbans, of silk for the women's *shelwars*, of prints of different designs and varying qualities for their tunics, and of chiffon for the head covers. Sometimes, to save money, a family may give most of the women white broadcloth instead of silk for *shelwars*.

Aziz, the older sister of Rafia, the girl who was to marry Phuphi's son's son. These two sisters were alone in the world; their parents had died and their relatives had remained in India. Now the older sister was marrying off the younger one, as if she were her mother. But as they had no relatives to give the older sister a *hath phareda*, Bebeji said to her: "You are my daughter," and gave her the necessary *jowṛa*.

Bebeji gave away these two outfits because of her close relationship with Phuphi. F.B. was Phuphi's son's wife, and the two girls were to become Phuphi's relatives by marriage. This action on Bebeji's part reflected her good *vartan bhanji* with Phuphi.

In the boy's house, on the day of *maiyañ*, the tying of the bracelet on the boy's wrist, the family gives *jowṛas* to the *kammi* women who work for the house. Usually there are seven of these outfits; they are of cotton and cost about 10 rupees.

At the time of the *meyl*, as the guests begin to arrive from the distant villages, the married sisters of the bridegroom bring him an outfit. They share the expenses of this *jowṛa*, and it is sewn and ready to be worn. The bridegroom wears it when he leaves with the *barat* for the bride's village. The *hath phareda*, the outfit received by the bridegroom's mother from her *peke* along with the clothes for her unmarried children and for her grandchildren, and the *jowṛa* received by the bridegroom from his married sisters are the only outfits received by the family of a boy who is getting married. The only exceptions are a *jowṛa* which the boy's *phuphi* may bring for him, but this would be of a quality inferior to that given by his married sisters, or a *jowṛa* brought for the boy by his father's brother's married daughters.

After the departure of the *barat*, when the guests are ready to leave, they are given *jowṛas* by the bridegroom's family. Women receive these as daughters of the house; among the recipients are included the following: *phuphi's* (father's sister's) married daughters and her sons' wives; father's brother's wife, daughters and sons' wives; mother's brother's wife (if mother's brother is younger than mother), his daughters and his sons' wives; mother's sisters (if they are younger than mother), their daughters and their sons' wives. Many other women also receive *jowṛas*, for the term "daughter of the house" can be extended to include almost every woman invited to the *meyl*.

Each of these women who has received a *jowṛa* will certainly be given outfits for her children and sometimes for her husband also. Whether or not a *jowṛa* is given to the husband of a daughter of the house depends on the closeness of the relationship as it is reflected in the *vartan bhanji* dealing.

The true daughters of the house (the bridegroom's married sisters and his father's sisters) stay on to see the bride. They leave only when the bride comes for her second visit, and before their departure each receives a *jowṛa* for herself and *jowṛas* for her husband, her unmarried daughters, and unmarried sons, and her husband's unmarried siblings.

At the marriage of a girl, the family receives a number of *jowṛas* for the bride from relatives and friends with whom they have this kind of *vartan bhanji*. On the day of the *maiyañ*, or immediately after, comes the bride's *nanke*, the household of her mother's parents, bringing *nanekwali*, the things given to a girl on her marriage by her mother's side. The gifts are brought by the mother's mother or, if she is not living, her mother's brothers' wives, who come with their husbands and children. The *nanekwali* includes three to five *jowṛas*, bedding, copperware, and golden ornaments. The bride's mother's married sisters are also *nanke*, but each of these brings one *jowṛa* for the bride on her own behalf.

Two days before the arrival of the *barat*, the *meylis*, wedding guests, arrive at the bride's house. These are relatives and close friends, and each household is represented by at least two women, one man, and some children. Each household brings a *jowṛa* for the bride, and the bride's married sisters and her father's sister each bring two. All these women are related to the bride by birth or marriage or are intimate friends of the family—in fact, they are all in the category of "daughters of the house," who have received or who will receive *jowṛas* from this family on an appropriate occasion, but whose turn it is now to give, for that is *vartan bhanji*. The women who are the donors include the following: father's brother's wife and daughters; father's sister's daughter; father's father's sister's daughters and sons' wives; father's father's brother's son's wife; father's father's father's brother's son's wife and his son's daughter; mother's sister's daughter and mother's brother's daughter, and so on. All these women who bring *jowṛas* for the bride and represent their households are married women or widows, for they alone can act in behalf of their households in *vartan bhanji*. An unmarried woman does not take an active part in *vartan bhanji*, that is, does not give away *jowṛas* or money or other articles of exchange, but she may be a recipient as a member of a household represented by a married woman or a widow.

At a girl's marriage, a family may receive twenty to thirty, or even more, *jowṛas*. Even the poorest *kammi* receives a number of *jowṛas*, usually of good quality. Each family makes an effort to maintain good *vartan bhanji* with as many families as possible, sometimes with even more than they can afford in terms of time and expense.

The jowṛas brought by all these women relatives and friends are given because of the *vartan bhanji* relationship between them and the bride's family. However, the *jowṛas* received from the *nanke* are not *vartan bhanji*; it is a daughter's daughter's right to receive *nanekwali* from her mother's side, and it is the duty of the *nanke* to give it. Nevertheless, this duty will be fulfilled only if a good relationship has been maintained between the respective families. In this case, the warm relationship itself is the *vartan bhanji*, which is expressed by bringing *nanekwali*, giving *hath phareda*, and fulfilling the other obligations to the daughter and the daughter's daughter. (The case of F.B., already described, illustrates the situation when no warm relationship had been fostered between the kin.)

At a girl's marriage, her family knows in advance how many *jowras* will be forthcoming. Bebeji likes to count the number of *jowras* which will be given at her young (unmarried) daughter's marriage. She remembers the *jowras* she herself has been giving for years on the marriage of daughters of relatives with whom she has *vartan bhanji*, which will now determine what will be given her daughter, "for that is how *vartan bhanji* goes." In addition to knowing the number, she also knows more or less what the quality will be in each case. She remembers well the quality of the *jowras* she has given, and also, through years of experience, she has learned the ways of each of her women partners. Some women have an established reputation for giving things of good quality, for dealing fairly in *vartan bhanji;* but a few are known for their meanness—they like to receive expensive *jowras* but try to deceive by giving *jowras* of gaudy, showy cloth of cheap quality. However, women are never deceived and they keep tally of everything given and everything received.

At the marriage of a girl, the family not only receives but also gives *jowras,* primarily to the sons-in-law of the house, their wives, and children. The first *jowra* is given to the bridegroom, the new son-in-law. He arrives with the *barat* wearing the clothes given him by his married sisters. If the *barat* leaves again on the same day, he changes into the clothes given by his parents-in-law, but if the *barat* stays overnight he puts on the new clothes on the following morning. The *jowra* given to the new son-in-law is not *vartan bhanji*. He is the daughter's husband, and receives the gift in terms of a daughter's right to receive from her father's house.

After the *barat* has departed with the bride, the wedding guests are ready to leave; the family then gives *jowras* to the other sons-in-law to make them feel that they are equally precious and important as the new son-in-law and also to enliven the existing relationship.

The actual sons-in-law are daughters' husbands and father's sisters' husbands, but the term *ghar da jivai,* sons-in-law of the house, may be extended to all the men married to daughters of the house in the extended sense of this term. Thus, those who may be given *jowras* include the husbands of the following women: daughter's daughter, son's daughter, father's sister's daughter, father's father's sister's daughter, and so on. However, how many *jowras* are given depends on the scale of the marriage, the lavishness of the spending, and also on previous events—that is, the actual sons-in-law may on earlier occasions have been given *jowras* by other families, who treated them as sons-in-law by extension of the term, and these gifts must now be reciprocated. *Jowras* may be given only to the husbands of true daughters and father's sisters. But if the family wishes to spend lavishly and to gain much prestige by giving, they will give *jowras* to all the men who, in the extended sense, are *ghar da jivai*. The *jowras* given to the husbands of true daughters and father's sisters are not *vartan bhanji*, but those given to the others are and they must be reciprocated on an appropriate occasion. At the same time, the family gives *jowras* to the wives of the sons-in-law (who are, of course, daughters and father's sisters) and their children.

When the bride comes to her husband's village with the *barat* she brings her dowry, her personal clothes, and *jowras* for all the members of her husband's family: his mother and father, his mother's mother, his father's mother and father, his father's sister, his married sisters, his married brothers and their wives, his unmarried sisters and brothers, and two *kammis* of the house. Later, on her second and third visits, she again brings *jowras* for her parents-in-law and their unmarried children.

Before the bride leaves, after her first visit to her parents-in-law, she receives two *jowras* from her mother-in-law and her relative who has come to escort the couple to her home is given one very good *jowra*.

Then, while the bridegroom is on his *muklawa* with the bride's parents, his father or both his parents come to fetch the couple and also to visit the bride's family for a day or two. If the families are

already related, they meet now in their new status of *kuṛum
kuṛumni,* parents of a married couple; if they are not related, this
is the time for them to become acquainted (for marriages usually
are arranged by a third party). The boy's parents are well entertained during their stay, and before they leave the girl's parents
give them expensive outfits and a substantial gift, such as a buffalo
or golden ornaments for the boy's mother. The girl is given two
or three *jowṛas* for herself, from her mother, and one *jowṛa* for her
husband. They take with them the outfits for the rest of the boy's
household.

Bebeji of Mohla and her husband went together to bring home
their oldest son, who was on his *muklawa* in Talwandi village. They
were served choice food and before leaving they were given very
good outfits by the mother of their new daughter-in-law. Bebeji's
youngest daughter, who was an infant, had been taken along, and
she was given clothes as were the two older children who were
left at home. The servant who accompanied them was given 10
rupees and a cotton blanket. Besides, Bebeji was presented with a
fine buffalo.

The flow of *jowṛas* from the parents of the bride to her new family during these initial visits is not *vartan bhanji.* It is a token given
in recognition of the fact that their parental authority has passed
over to the parents-in-law who are now the bride's parents. When
the bride is seated in her *ḍowli,* palanquin, the whole family
weeps and they say, "Now we have no more authority over her."
The gifts are intended also to establish a good relationship for the
daughter in the family of her parents-in-law, to build up her prestige in her new home, and to create a tie between the two families.
Should this connection be maintained, it leads to *vartan bhanji*
and closer ties.

This may be illustrated by an actual case. Bebeji married her
older son to a girl from Talwandi Village. Some time after N.B.,
the daughter-in-law, had settled down in her new home, her father's brother's daughter, who was married in a nearby village,

passed through Mohla and stopped to visit her. When she was leaving, Bebeji, after having consulted N.B., presented the visitor with a *jowra* and gave 10 and 5 rupees, respectively, to her husband's youngest sister and her child, who had come with her.

By making these gifts, Bebeji was making it plain that her new daughter-in-law and her relatives were welcome in this house. At the same time, Bebeji was opening the way for N.B., as a married woman, to begin *vartan bhanji* with her own relatives.

Not long after, N.B.'s father's father's brother's son's daughter was to be married in Talwandi. Bebeji, N.B., and the whole household were invited from Mohla. At a girl's marriage, her married sisters bring her *jowras;* in the extended meaning of the term, N.B. was a "sister" of the bride. So Bebeji, N.B., and her husband, and Bebeji's youngest children went to the wedding, taking with them the gifts—*jowras* and sweets. Before they returned, N.B.'s husband was given a *jowra* as a son-in-law of the house, N.B. received a *jowra* as a daughter of the house, and Bebeji's young children were given *jowras*.

In the meantime, N.B. went on her customary visits to her *peke*, parents' household, once or twice a year. Each time she returned she would bring *jowras* for herself, for her husband and children, and also for her husband's younger brother and sisters in the same household, and sweets. The gifts she received from her parents for herself, her husband, and her children were given as a daughter's right; but the *jowras* for the younger members of the household were an indication of the pleasant relationship established between her parents and her parents-in-law.

Then the marriage of N.B.'s younger sister took place. Bebeji and N.B. went to Talwandi to attend the wedding, taking *jowras* for the bride and sweets. Since they lived in a joint household, the income of which was managed by Bebeji as its head, it was only with Bebeji's consent and approval that N.B. could take *jowras* for her sister. By attending her sister's marriage and taking gifts for her, two main purposes were achieved: first, *vartan bhanji* was established between Bebeji's household and that of her daughter-in-law's parents; secondly, N.B. took the initial steps in establishing her own *vartan bhanji* relationship with her sister.

In this way, during the seventeen years of N.B.'s marriage, a number of events—births, circumcisions, marriages, illnesses, deaths —took place among the relatives on her parents' side and among the relatives on her husband's side. These occasions were attended, and the customary gifts were exchanged. Thus, N.B. was able to establish her own *vartan bhanji* with the relatives on her parents' side and, at the same time, through her, the household of her parents-in-law and most of their relatives were introduced to her parents and their relatives and *vartan bhanji* relations were established between the two sides.

MONEY

Money has an important place and is widely used in *vartan bhanji* in two different ways. First, all important ceremonies call for the giving of money, and, second, any of the articles used— sweets, dry food, *jowṛas*—may be substituted with money under certain conditions. When money is given as a substitute, the amount given should be equivalent to the value of the customary article.

At the marriage of a girl, for example, relatives and friends bring *jowṛas* and sweets. If they bring the *jowṛas* but no sweets, they will give money as a substitute for the sweets; if they bring neither of these gifts, they will give the amount of money needed to buy the kind of *jowṛa* and the amount of sweets they should have brought. Or when dry food is sent to the house of marriage by a friend or a *biraderi*, if any of the items is lacking from the required combination, its equivalent in money will be sent. If vermicelli, *ghi*, and sugar—one of the combinations used in *vartan bhanji*—should be sent, but either *ghi* or sugar, or both of these, are lacking, then vermicelli and money will be sent. Or it may happen that a family, who has to give a *jowṛa* to a visiting relative, does not have on hand the required three unsewn pieces of cloth. If they have the two pieces of cloth needed for the *shelwar* and the tunic, they will give these and add money for the headcloth; alternatively, they may give the sum of money needed for a complete *jowṛa*.

However, money may replace an article of *vartan bhanji* only under certain conditions. For example, after a wedding, the house of marriage should give sweets to the departing guests; these cannot be replaced by money. If for some inexplicable reason, there are not enough sweets, they will still owe sweets to the family who were to receive them. If money is to be substituted for an article of exchange, there must be a legitimate reason for doing so. For example, a person who is coming to participate in some special event may have been under pressure of time and so have been unable to purchase the article. Or a visiting relative may have come unexpectedly and only for a short stay; then if the family does not have on hand an appropriate *jowṛa* and does not have time to purchase one, they may give money instead. Or when dry food is sent, money may replace a missing item if, for instance, refined sugar is rationed at the time or if, as happens at certain periods of the year, there is a shortage of *ghi*. However, marriages are planned long in advance and a family who is celebrating a marriage should be fully prepared to perform the required ceremonies and to give away cloth and sweets; therefore, in their case, money cannot be used as a substitute.

Money is given as *vartan bhanji* on all important occasions—birth, circumcision, marriage, sickness, and the death of an old person. In connection with marriage, the ceremonies which call for the giving of money by relatives and friends as part of *vartan bhanji* begin with the sending of the wedding invitations and end at the time of the bride's second visit to her parents-in-law.

The family of a girl and of a boy who are inviting guests to a marriage sends a messenger to important relatives and close friends who live within a distance of some fifty miles. This messenger delivers the invitation orally and also brings a present of *ptassa*, sugar candy. The woman at the head of each household to which the message is delivered then gives some money to the messenger. This money—2, 3, 5, 7, 9, or 11 rupees—is called *vedaigi,* money given to a *kammi* who has brought a wedding invitation. It counts toward the *vartan bhanji* between the two households and will be reciprocated. Upon his return home, the *kammi* informs the house of marriage how much he has received as *vedaigi* from the several households to which he has delivered invitations. The *kammi* keeps the money, it is his; but the amount given to him by each household is recorded in the family register, the *vehi,* and will be credited to the family who gave it. At the wedding, the relatives who gave *vedaigi* may bring along a *kammi* of their own house. Before they depart, the woman who is the head of the house of marriage will give money to the visitors' *kammi.* Should she neglect to give back the *vedaigi,* the guest will remind her by saying: "Give my *vedaigi* to my *kammi.*" The hostess may give the same amount, a little less or a little more.

About a week before the *barat,* at the ceremony of *maiyañ,* where a bracelet of colored thread is tied around the wrist of the bridegroom, the wife or mother of the barber who is the *kammi* of the house passes around a bowl with a little oil in it. First the mother of the bridegroom drops in a coin; that is from the house. Then some of the women attending the ceremony follow suit. These women are *biraderis* of the village and some other village women who are on the level of *vartan bhanji* with the family in which money is exchanged. The head of the house watches how much money each woman gives, but if the gathering is so large that the hostess cannot see, either the woman carrying the bowl or the woman giving the money will inform her of the amount. Usually a woman, as she drops the coin into the bowl, will say to the hostess: "This much is yours, and this extra money is mine." The "extra money" represents the amount in excess of what the hostess has given on a similar occasion. This money, given at *maiyañ* by the women who have *vartan bhanji* with the family, is called *chowl* and is for the barber's wife or mother; on some later occasion it will be reciprocated. The amount given by each woman varies from 2 annas (16 annas equals one rupee) to one rupee, and the total amount of *chowl* collected at a *maiyañ* is at most 10 rupees. The same ceremony takes place in the household of the bride.

The next ceremony at which money is given is the *khara*, the ceremony in which the bridegroom ritually bathes before he puts on the wedding outfit brought by his married sisters. It takes place on the day the *barat* leaves for the bride's village. On this occasion, the bridegroom receives *khara lhai*, a present "to get off the washing plank." Amid all the women relatives, the bridegroom takes his bath standing on a washing plank. The lower part of his body is wrapped in an old *lungi*, wrap-around sheet, which he will give to the barber who, together with the potter's wife, assists him. When he has finished washing, before he may step off the plank, he must be given a gift by his *nanke*, which is presented by his mother's brother or, if he is not living, his mother's brother's son. This gift is called *khara lhai* and it may be money, a buffalo, or a horse. Besides his *nanke,* his father's brother and his father's sister's husband may give him money as *khara lhai*. The gift received from his *nanke* is not *vartan bhanji*, for it is his mother's right in her parents' home to have *khara lhai* given to her son. However, the money received from the father's brother and the father's sister's husband is *vartan bhanji,* and his parents will have to reciprocate on a similar occasion. The bridegroom may keep the money given as *khara lhai*, but if he feels that his parents are in need because of the wedding expenses, he will give it to them.

While the bridegroom receives his *khara lhai*, the barber passes around a bowl with a little buttermilk at the bottom. The mother or the father's mother is the first to drop in a coin; that is from the house. Then the women present, all of whom belong to the restricted circle of those who deal fully in *vartan bhanji* with the family, follow suit and inform the mistress of the house how much they have given. This money, given at the *khara* ceremony, is called *chowl* and is for the barber and the other *kammi* who have assisted the bridegroom. It is counted as *vartan bhanji* and will be reciprocated on an appropriate occasion.

The ceremony of *khara* is performed for the bride also. She takes her ritual bath on the day she is to leave with the bridegroom for his village, for the *barat* usually arrives in the late afternoon, stays overnight, and leaves the next day. While taking her bath, the girl squats on a washing plank, her knees drawn up to hide her breasts and the lower part of her body wrapped in an old *lungi*, which is given to the barber's wife who assists her. The bride receives *khara lhai*. *Chowl* is collected and is given to the barber's wife. After the bath, the bride puts on the bridal clothes and ornaments brought by the *barat* from her parents-in-law.

After the *khara*, the bridegroom puts on the clothes given him by his married sisters and a turban with a veil of fresh flowers that covers his face. Then he sits among the women who are attending the wedding. Now he receives *selami*, "welcome" money. First his mother gives him 5 or 10 rupees as *selami* from his own house. Then all the married women who belong in the category of daughter of the house give him *selami*—his father's brother's wife, his father's sister, his mother's brother's wife, his mother's sister, his married sisters, and so on. It is said that formerly people gave as *selami* only 1 or 2 rupees, but nowadays people give 5, 10, or 20 rupees (if they are very wealthy). Only women give *selami* to the bridegroom. While they are doing so, his mother, or the wife of his elder brother, or some other responsible woman of the *biraderi* stands close by to watch and remember how much each woman gives, for except for that given by his mother and his married sisters, this is *vartan bhanji* and must be reciprocated. *Selami* welcomes the boy in his new status as a bridegroom; he may keep the money or give it to his parents if they need it.

While the women are giving *selami*, the men are outside in the men's section of the house collecting *neondra*. *Neondra* is the money collected by the parents of the bridegroom at his wedding. *Neondra* is given by men—the relatives and close friends who are invited to the wedding and who have *vartan bhanji* with the family. A poor *kammi* gives 1 to 10 rupees; a rich *kammi* or a well-to-do *zamindar* gives 5 to 101 rupees. *Neondra* is collected shortly before the bridegroom leaves with the *barat*. The bridegroom's father, father's brother, or some other responsible member of the *biraderi* sits down on a cot with a large tray covered with a cloth by his side. Nearby sits the scribe, or the village *imam,* or some member of the *biraderi* who can write. A handful of sugar is placed on the tray, and the first money is given by the house. Then the relatives and friends come up one by one to give money to the man in charge of its collection. The scribe registers the amount given in the family register, the *vehi*. The sum collected as *neondra* helps the family to cover a part of the cost of the marriage.

At the wedding of A.M., a *zamindar* of Mohla, his older brother came to borrow money from the *chowdhri*. In the midst of the marriage celebrations, the household had run short of money. A.M.'s brother promised repayment after the family had collected *neondra,* but he could do so only in part because the sum collected—800 rupees—was less than they had expected.

People who are invited to a boy's wedding usually inquire beforehand whether or not the family intends to collect *neondra,* so they may come prepared. Parents who want to gain much *izzet,* prestige, accept very little *neondra*. The guests may give 101 rupees, but the family accepts only 5 rupees and returns the rest. The money retained is merely a token of having *vartan bhanji* with the donor.

Neondra is not collected at a girl's wedding.

It is noteworthy that whereas almost every other aspect of dealing in *vartan bhanji* is attended to only by women, only men give and collect *neondra*.

In the bridegroom's house, after *selami* and *neondra* have been collected, it is time for the *barat* to leave. The bridegroom is still among the women. Now he stands up, ready to go. All the women surround him. One by one, each woman takes out some money and, holding it in her hand, turns it around his head and gives it to a member of a household who is standing nearby, watching and remembering how much each woman has given. The bridegroom's mother or father's mother gives the first money from the house. The other women, all the daughters of the house follow her. This is the ceremony of *serwarna*, turning over the head. Well-to-do people usually give 1 or 2 rupees; the poor give half a rupee. The money collected is given to the poorest of the *kammi* women who work for the house, who have not received much during the other marriage ceremonies. Money given at *serwarna* is *vartan bhanji* and will be reciprocated.

Now the bridegroom mounts his horse. The *baratis*, the men who go in the marriage procession, have mounted their horses. The barber carries the box containing *varasui*, presents of clothes and ornaments for the bride. But the bridegroom cannot move. His sisters, married and unmarried, and his cousins—father's brother's daughter, mother's brother's daughter, father's sister's daughter, mother's sister's daughter, all those with whose families a close relationship is maintained—hang onto the reins of his horse. He gives them money and they let him go. This money is called *vag pharai*, holding the reins. Usually the bridegroom gives 10 rupees to each woman. This money is *vartan bhanji* and will be reciprocated.

Other money given at a wedding is *veyl*, money given by men to the *mirasis*, the village bards, who entertain the male guests. Whenever there is a wedding, the village bards of the surrounding area ask permission of the house of marriage to sing and play music for their guests. They come to the bridegroom's house one day before the departure of the *barat*.

As the *mirasis* sing and play, listeners who enjoy the music and wish to honor the house of marriage give them money. Each time the musicians receive money, they stop playing and one of them sings out the name of the donor, the name of his village, and the amount he has given, and finally he extolls the virtues of the house of marriage in whose honor the money has been given. The music

and singing begin again, but are soon interrupted by another dona-
tion. The donors are members of the *biraderi*, other relatives,
friends, people who work for the house, and some *kammis* and
zamindars of the village, all of whom have *vartan bhanji* with the
family. The amount given by each man is 1, 2, or 5 rupees; what
he has given is reported to the women of the house, who will remember it well, for it must be reciprocated.

The *mirasis* also come from the surrounding villages to entertain
the male guests at the girl's wedding. They come the day before
the *barat* arrives and stay until the bride leaves. Here, too, they
are given *veyl* by the members of the *biraderi* of the girl's family,
other relatives, and friends; it is part of *vartan bhanji*.

After the *barat* has left the bridegroom's home, the guests make
ready to leave for their own homes, but they wait to see the valuable gifts which the married sisters of the bridegroom and the
father's sister will receive from the parental house. Each one of
these women is given a buffalo, or golden ornaments, or 100 to 300
rupees. If the father's brother's daughter brought an outfit for the
bridegroom, she receives 100 rupees. The guests also receive their
gifts of clothes and sweets, which are part of their *vartan bhanji*
with the family, and go their way. Of all the guests, now only the
married sisters, father's sister, and the *nanke*, mother's mother and
mother's brother's wife, remain, waiting for the bride's arrival.

At the bride's house there are no ceremonies corresponding to
sevarna or to *vag pharai*, but *selami* is given both to the bridegroom and to the bride.

The *barat* arrives at the bride's house in the afternoon. *Nikah*,
the ceremony of the marriage contract, is performed, and food is
served to the guests. On the following day, before the bridegroom
meets the bride for the first time, he dresses in the clothes prepared
for him by the bride's house and then he is brought into the
women's section of the house, where he sits among the women to
receive *selami* from them. First, as *selami* from his parents-in-law,

his mother-in-law gives him money, 5 to 100 rupees, depending upon the family's status. She is followed by all the other women relatives and friends who have *vartan bhanji* with the bride's family—the bride's father's sister, mother's sister, father's brother's wife, mother's brother's wife, father's brother's daughter, the married sisters, and all the daughters of the house. Each gives 5 to 10 rupees, or, among the poor, 1 to 2 rupees. The bridegroom keeps the money he has received as *selami* in the bride's house, for it is his money, or he may give it to his parents if they are in need. But while it is being given, a responsible woman of the household watches and remembers how much each woman has given, for this money must be reciprocated by the household of the bride. After he has received *selami*, the bridegroom joins the male guests.

While the *barat* is in the bride's village, three ceremonies may be performed by men of the bridegroom's family which establish—or strengthen—connections between the bridegroom's family and village, on the one hand, and the family and village of the bride and other villages, on the other.[9] The first is a ceremony in which the bridegroom's family distributes *thehan*, presents of copper plates filled with sweets and also money, to the married daughters and daughters' daughters of the bridegroom's subcaste and village living in the bride's village. The recipients of *thehan* are among the women who give *selami* to the bridegroom. The second is the ceremony of *ratha chari* in which the bridegroom's family distributes money to *mirasis*, bards, from other villages, particularly from those villages whose daughters and daughters' daughters are married into the bridegroom's village. The third is that in which a sum of money, known as *chul*, is distributed to all the households of *kammis* in the bride's village.

Then comes the time when the bride is to leave with the *barat*. Dressed in the clothes and ornaments brought by the bridegroom,

---

[9] A more detailed description of these ceremonies is given above, in Chapter XI.

she is seated in a *dowli,* palanquin. Here she receives *selami,* first from her own household as her mother (or father's mother or brother's wife) gives her 5 or 10 rupees, and then from all the women relatives—father's sister, mother's sister, father's brother's wife, mother's brother's wife, her married sisters, her father's brother's daughter—and all the women who are daughters of the house. Besides these women, the wives of *kammis* and of *zamindars* in the village who have *vartan bhanji* with the family also give *selami* to the bride. The amount given may be 1, 2, 5, or 10 rupees. One of the bride's married sisters or her brother's wife stands near the *dowli* to watch and to remind the bride to remember how much she was given by each woman, for this money will be reciprocated by the bride's household. The money belongs to the bride; usually she has golden ornaments made with it, but sometimes she may give it to her parents. The giving of *selami* to the bride in the village of her parents completes the giving of money at ceremonies there.

After the bride has left with the *barat,* the guests receive their presents of sweets and clothes, and make ready to go to their homes.

Immediately upon her arrival in the bridegroom's village, the bride receives *selami* from her mother-in-law or, if she is not living, from the bridegroom's older brother's wife. The amount of money she gives is from 5 or 10 up to 100 rupees, depending upon the status of the family. Then the bridegroom's *nanke,* his married sisters and his father's sister, who have stayed behind to welcome the bride, give her *selami.* Each woman gives her 5 or 10 rupees. This money belongs to the bride and she may keep it, or she may give it to her mother-in-law.

Now the *nanke* and father's sister leave, but the bridegroom's married sisters will remain with their parents until the bride returns for her second visit. Then they, too, will return home, taking their presents with them. This completes the giving of money.

In describing the various articles—sweets, food, yard goods, and money—which are distributed as *vartan bhanji* during the ceremonies connected with marriage and on other occasions, reference has also been made to other types of valuable gifts. These include such things as the articles which form part of the bride's dowry—bedding, copper and brassware, and so on—and buffaloes or horses, and gold ornaments. Although all these valuables are gifts associated with such events as marriage, they should be clearly distinguished from the gifts which are *vartan bhanji*.

These valuable gifts are given only on specific important occasions (in this case, marriage); they are given by very close relatives (such as the mother's or father's brother, or the bridegroom's sisters, or the parents of the bride or bridegroom) to the central figures in the event (the bride, the bridegroom, the sisters of the bridegroom, the parents of the bride or the bridegroom); and they are not reciprocated. Like the gifts exchanged in *vartan bhanji*, they establish or strengthen ties between two people—or, actually, between two groups of people—emphasizing the relationship between them, and they are the forerunners of other gifts on other occasions. Where a new connection is made (as, at a marriage, between the families of the bride and bridegroom) these presents are, as it were, indicators of possible *vartan bhanji*, but they are not themselves *vartan bhanji*. That is, the valuable presents given by the family of the bride to the bridegroom and his parents, and *vice versa*, are indirect indicators of the *vartan bhanji* relations that will be established between members of the two families and their relatives, but they are not *vartan bhanji*.

Besides valuables, such as buffaloes and gold ornaments, some of the types of articles given as *vartan bhanji*, particularly yard goods and money, also belong in this category of gifts when given

[10] There is no collective term in Punjabi for the gifts included here as "valuables."

or received by certain individuals. So, for example, the outfit given as *hath phareda* to the mothers of the bride and bridegroom, to each by her *peke,* or the outfit given to the bridegroom, together with a gold ring, by his sisters, and money given to the bride and the bridegroom as *khara lhai,* to each by the mother's brother, or money, buffalo, or gold ornaments given by the bride's parents to the bridegroom's mother at the time of the ceremonial visit to the bride's house and village—all of these fall into the category of gifts now discussed.

The giving of these gifts follows the pattern of the dowry, and many of the gifts given and received are, in fact, phrased as being part of a daughter's right. Thus it is a daughter's right to receive part of her daughter's dowry from her parents (the bride's *nanke*); it is a sister's right to be given valuable presents by her parents at the marriage of her brother; it is a daughter's right that her son or daughter receive valuable presents as *khara lhai* from her brother, and so on.

In considering the presents given and received at a ceremony such as a marriage, it is therefore necessary, on the one hand, to distinguish between those given and received as *vartan bhanji* and those which it is an individual's duty to give and right to receive and, on the other hand, to distinguish three levels of giving—the presents given to the widest circle (mainly sweets and food), those given to relatives and close friends (sweets, food, *jowras,* and money), and those given within the small circle of closely related kin (sweets, food, *jowras,* money, and various sorts of valuables).

XVII

The Focus of Giving

In the preceding chapter, the articles have been enumerated which are distributed and received by the households of the bride and the bridegroom on the occasion of a wedding. Sweets, food, cloth for *jowras*, and money are exchanged on a very large scale even in the poorest household. The nature of the article, the ceremony at which it is given and received, and the categories of individuals who are donors and recipients at each step are fixed by custom. While some acts of giving are matters of individual choice (for instance, a father's brother may or may not give his nephew a *jowra* in addition to the one given by the bridegroom's married sisters) individual latitude is primarily a matter of scale. That is, there are permissible differences in the costliness of an article as well as in the number of persons who, especially by an extended use of kinship terms, may be recipients and donors, even though the nature of the article and the category of the person are fixed by custom and the scale of performance is in part determined by customary attitudes toward social status.

One important feature of these exchanges is that, where specific partners are concerned, the scale of performance is determined neither by the donor nor by the recipient alone but by mutual consent. Not only may a donor take initiative in giving but a recipient may, on the one hand, criticize a gift as inadequate or, on the other hand, decide not to accept a gift—or he may set a limit to lavishness by returning some part of it—on the grounds that the

pressure for return will be too great. As the individual recipient—
who on other occasions is a donor—can set a brake on how much
is given, lavishness in giving involves the extension of giving to
many persons and this, in turn, increases the number of individuals
who, on other occasions, will be donors vis-à-vis a particular individual or, more exactly, household. Furthermore, giving and receiving enhance the prestige not of one but of both participants. So,
for instance, when the male guests give *veyl* to the *mirasis*, the
village bards, both the donor and the household which is honored
are praised by a singer.

A second important feature of these exchanges is that, while the
same individual may on a particular occasion be at one moment a
donor and at another a recipient vis-à-vis another individual, these
transactions do not cancel each other out; rather, each can be returned only in its own kind and on a parallel occasion—sweets given
to the departing wedding guests must be returned as sweets on a
like occasion; *jowṛas* brought to a bride must be returned as *jowṛas*
for another bride.[1] So the partners in exchange are involved not
in single transactions which could be written off at any point in
their entirety but in a related set of many transactions the completion of which is necessarily spread out over many years and is
determined in part by circumstances outside the control of the
individuals; for instance, a gift given to a bride at the time of her
marriage can be reciprocated only when one's own daughter's
marriage ceremonies take place. Yet, at the same time, the attitude
of the partners in exchange as it is expressed in behavior on any
one occasion spreads to all others as, through exchange, a relationship becomes close and warm or, on the contrary, becomes increasingly formal and perfunctory. To remain alive, the exchange
must continually be enlivened.

The continuous activities of mature women, wives, or widows

---

[1] But balance in the system as a whole is somewhat protected by having permissible substitutions, for example, where a family has no daughter or where
the customary donor is, for some reason, lacking.

who are the heads and representatives of households, as the principal mediators in the exchange of gifts indicate the importance of women as the central figures in carrying on *vartan bhanji*. Men take an active part in exchange only in the most limited way in the ceremonies connected with marriage—in the giving of *khara lhai* by the mother's brother, in the giving and receiving of *neondra*, in the giving and receiving of *veyl*, and in the giving of money by the bridegroom to his sisters and cousins at the ceremony of *vag pharai*. Thus, while a household is ultimately dependent upon men to supply the wherewithal to carry on gift exchange and while the scale of exchange is determined in part by the status of men, the actual functioning of the exchange and the enhancement of household prestige depend upon the skills of women. In this, as in other aspects of the whole mechanism of exchange, division of activity has the effect of emphasizing joint responsibility in the achievement of a goal.

However, the most important point to note in all these exchanges is the category of persons on whom the giving focuses. For the primary recipients are the daughters—the true daughters—of the house and the father's sisters, and then, by extension, all those who come to be regarded as daughters or as father's sisters.

On every occasion, a daughter receives because it is *her right to receive from her father's house*. At the marriage of her son, she receives from her parents *hath phareda* for herself, clothes for her whole family and for the children of her married daughters and sons, and from her brother *khara lhai* for her son, and sweets. At the marriage of her daughter, she receives clothes for herself, *nanek-wali* and *khara lhai* for her daughter, and sweets. At the wedding of her brother and at the birth of his son, she receives clothes for herself and her family, a buffalo or golden ornaments, and sweets. At the marriage of her sister, her husband receives clothes as the husband of the daughter, and she herself and her children receive clothes. If her husband dies during her lifetime, she receives clothes for the whole family and shrouds for the deceased; if he dies after she does, he still gets the shrouds. If her children die, they are given shrouds and an outfit to be given away. When her parents-in-law die, she is given outfits for herself, her husband and children, and for all the members of her husband's household. At the marriage of her brother's son, she receives clothes and a buffalo as the sister of the father (or as a daughter of the house), and she is given gifts again at the birth of her brother's son's son. On all important occasions, she receives gifts, for this is her right.

Thus in *vartan bhanji*—in this relationship which binds together near kin, distant kin, blood and affinal kin, the served and the server, individuals of the same status and individuals of different status, members of one caste and members of different castes, neighbors within a village and the inhabitants of neighboring villages, and which, on important occasions, brings together representatives of all these different categories of partners—the key figure is the daughter who, as a married adult, is simultaneously the daughter-in-law in another family. She is the connecting link between the two families she represents.

There is a crucial difference between the true daughter and the daughter of the house in the extended meaning of this term. Both the true daughter and the daughter of the house by extension are focal points of giving. But whereas the true daughter (or the father's true sister) receives as her right and reciprocates very little, the households of daughters of the house must reciprocate in full measure whatever has been given. By giving to the daughters of the house, families establish and maintain relationships with all their relatives, blood and affinal, to whose households all these women, as true daughters, belong, and for whom, therefore, reciprocation must be made to those who gave to them as daughters in the extended meaning of the term.

The pattern of giving and receiving outside the kin group reinforces and is reinforced by parallel relationships of reciprocity existing among nonkin, though what is given and received is modified to suit the requirements of the degree of intimacy and also the

specific type of relationship; for instance, what is exchanged between *zamindar* and *kammi* or between two *kammis* is determined, among other things, by whether or not the *kammi* is one
of those who works for a house as well as by his particular craft—
barber or agricultural laborer.

The mutual strengthening of particular ties and of all existing
ties is ensured by the occurrence and recurrence of important occasions when a very wide range of people is brought together, for
then, at some time and to some degree, no one in the village is left
out. People say: "Joy and sorrow are the occasions for coming
together." Otherwise, once an occasion is missed, a rift may occur
which, with time, may grow wider. Thus every event is an occasion
to renew and strengthen relationships, and *vartan bhanji* is the way
to do it.

Epilogue: Mohla in a Changing World, 1949–1955

In the villages, well-to-do people and those who through ownership of land and other property have had more contact with officials and influential people from outside have had greater opportunities to become modernized than the rest. But with modernization, well-to-do people do not permanently leave their villages. Those who go into politics attend meetings and important government sessions, but afterward return home to their villages because their lands are there, and the sources of their power are in the villages and in intervillage connections. Those who go into business may be away in another province for months, but their families remain in the village with the father or an elderly brother. As brothers and close *biraderi* become partners in business, each man returns to his home in turn while the rest carry on the work. Most of those who are in government service or who have professions that require their residence in a city—physicians and engineers—continue to maintain their homes and keep their families in the villages, where they go on important occasions, on weekends, and for vacations. They have a house in the village, and often build a new and better one; they expect to retire to the village and want to keep alive their connections with village people. Because they bring to their village houses whatever improvements are available in the cities, there is little gap between city life and the life of well-to-do people in the village.

Among the village people, the *kammis*—particularly the members of some castes—have been alert to some kinds of innovation because, in fact, their occupations had been affected by innovation long before the partition. Many of them have had to compete with foreign manufactured goods brought into the country by the British since the latter part of the nineteenth century. As a result, certain types of village craftsmen—the dyer, the oilsman, the silversmith, the weaver—who formerly were among the essential *kammis* are nowadays not found in every village.

Few people in Mohla remember the time when a weaver was one of the *kammis* of the house. As prestige was attached to the use of manufactured cloth introduced by the British, the services of the weaver were no longer wholly indispensable. However, his work is still needed because people prefer native cloth for rough use and for bedding because it is much stronger than imported cloth, and also because he weaves the cotton blankets which are part of a girl's dowry of bedding, are worn as shawls by men, and are given to *kammis* on ceremonial occasions. So, over a long period, the handweaver's work was modified in the villages, but the need for it has not been superseded.

Certain innovations have been discarded as unsuccessful. For example, in the 1940's, improved handlooms were introduced in the cities on which strips of cloth 45 inches wide—instead of 18 inches wide as on the traditional looms—could be woven. Of the eleven families of weavers in Mohla, two acquired these new looms and set them up in their homes. On a visit to relatives in Jelalpur Jatan—a city ten miles from Mohla which is a center of the weaving industry—these two weavers had seen the new looms. On the advice of their relatives, they learned their use and brought them to their own village. On the new looms they used machine-spun thread, the distribution of which was controlled and which could be obtained only from the Yarn Syndicate or from textile factories. The weaver wove the cloth at home and sold it at the market price. However, the rise and fall of market prices, competition with cloth manufactured by power looms in textile plants, and frequent changes in government policy proved to be more than village weavers could cope with. After a while, the two weavers went back to their traditional looms, and no more of the new looms appeared in the village. However, they did not discard the new looms and even now use them occasionally. All the weavers in Mohla have the desire to learn new things and to use modern techniques so as to meet the demands of changing fashions. But in the meantime the old looms continue in use.

In somewhat the same way as the weaver, other craftsmen have been affected in various ways by innovations and changes over a longer period. Through these they have acquired a differential awareness of new things and of the world beyond the village horizon.

Both the village barber and the bards, the *mirasis*, have been well aware that they live in a changing world. The barber is a man who has traveled to other villages and to cities in his capacity as a messenger. As receptionists both the barber and the *mirasi* hear the talk among the guests who come to their village—among them officials and well-educated people. As matchmakers they both are aware of changing demands by families who are looking for a bride or a bridegroom. As an entertainer, the *mirasi* is always present at weddings and has detailed information about the status of the different families, their children, and their manner of living. So their traditional roles have made all the *biraderis* of barbers and bards sensitive to even small changes that affect their clients and themselves.

The carpenter, the blacksmith, the cobbler, and the potter are the craftsmen whose work formerly was most closely connected with agriculture. A carpenter used to make and repair the plough and the yoke and all the woodwork required for the Persian wheel. He also did the necessary woodwork in house construction and the elaborate carving on doors, window shutters, closet doors, and on the central pillar in the main room of the house. In addition, he

made cots and stools, spinning wheels, churning sticks, hand ginning machines, and the large and small wooden boxes in which the
dowry of the bride was packed. Formerly, two carpenter families
served Mohla and the two neighboring villages, and they had full-
time work all the year round. Within the last twenty years, however, the woodwork on the Persian wheel has been replaced by
ready-made iron equipment which can be bought in the city. The
plough and other wooden objects—cots, stools, churning sticks, and
so on—can be obtained in the markets. Since the timber used in
construction can now be bought in lumber yards, where it is sawn
on machines, the carpenter spends less time than before on house
construction. The central pillar is no longer used and there is no
more demand for elaborate carving. The wooden boxes have been
replaced by tin boxes, and well-to-do *zamindars* give their daughters at least one suit case in which to pack their best clothes and
jewelry.

The demand for better agricultural equipment came through the
efforts of the Department of Agriculture, which demonstrated the
use of the improved plough in the villages. As to furniture, people
saw better things in the cities and the village carpenter had to
keep his trade up to date. Many carpenters began to specialize in
the things they made best; thus one made spinning wheels and
another ploughs, which could then be bought only in certain villages. Or a carpenter would make several spinning wheels and sell
them as he went through a village on a bicycle. So the demand for
better products resulted in more intense specialization.

Of the two families of carpenters in Mohla, the head of one
family is constantly away. He is now in his thirties and has had a
primary school education in the village school. While he was still
a young boy, his father sent him to his maternal uncle who worked
in a furniture store in the city of Gujrat, where he learned how to
make city furniture. After that he worked in the village for a time,
but as there was not enough work he left for the city where he now
does construction work. When his older son completed primary

school, he joined his father to learn the trade. Mohla's other carpenter is able to carry on with the work of three villages. His oldest son works with him, but the younger sons go to school.

All carpenters now learn masonry work. A few carpenters and blacksmiths who have money have opened flour mills in the villages; some have *zamindars* as partners in their enterprise. Others have opened furniture stores in the city. But no matter where they work, they maintain their families in the village.

In the same way, the potters have become specialists. The potters in the village of Shadiwal have specialized in making large flat bowls for kneading dough, for which the clay found in this locality seems to be particularly well suited. Whoever goes to that village brings a few back for friends and relatives, and so the bowls of Shadiwal travel 150 miles or more. The village of Kalra, near Gujrat, has specialized in churning pots, and the city of Gujrat is famous for its fine drinking bowls, which are associated in name with the romantic poem "Sohni Mehiñwal" as they are called "the bowls of Sohni," after the heroine.

Formerly, the potter had a great deal of work in connection with the Persian wheel, since earthenware buckets were used. A small village whose lands are irrigated by wells has eight or ten wells, and one hundred buckets are needed for each. It took the potter months to prepare these buckets; as they were breakable, he had to make two hundred or more for each well. However, in the last twenty years people have come to use iron buckets, which can be bought in the city.

Formerly, also, the potter made most of the housewares—dishes, drinking bowls, cooking pots, churning pots, and so on. He also made *kuzas*, small water vessels used in ablutions, for pouring water on the hands of a guest before and after meals, and for washing one's hands and face. A number of *kuzas* were provided for the mosque. Additionally, he made *hukas*, hubble bubble, and the small containers used as oil lamps in the houses and the mosque.

But in the last ten years, cheap, mass-produced, metal alloy utensils have become available. The *kuzas* have been replaced by *lotas*—metal vessels of the same shape; brass and copper *lotas* had already long been in use in well-to-do homes. *Hukas* are made of metal or of metal combined with wood or leather. Metal containers have replaced earthenware for lamps. Brass and copper plates have replaced earthenware plates and drinking bowls; large brass pitchers also are manufactured but have not become popular. People buy them for the dowry but use them to store sugar, *ghi,* and other provisions. For daily use they still prefer earthenware for milk and water pitchers, churning pots, kneading bowls, and for certain cooking pots. Recently, crockery plates, water glasses, and tea and water sets have become fashionable among well-to-do *zamindars,* and prestige is attached to their use for guests.

Thus the potter, whose work has been reduced, specializes in making certain wares not easy to get outside the village. Besides, he has acquired mules and horses and in his spare time transports grain from the fields to the house, the market, or the flour mill. He also transports construction materials. Sometimes he himself buys agricultural products—wheat, straw, fodder—and takes them to the city to sell. Some potters have gone into the ceramic factories which have opened in the cities and have learned new techniques.

The blacksmith formerly made ploughshares and such small agricultural implements as hoes and scythes. He also made padlocks and chains for the houses and chains for tethering buffaloes and did repair work on the Persian wheels. For a long time now, ploughshares, agricultural implements, padlocks, and chains have been sold in the city markets, but many people still prefer to have them made by the village blacksmith. His work on the Persian wheel was increased by the change from earthenware to iron buckets. Although hand pumps have been known in the villages for thirty years, they have come into increased use only in the last fifteen years. In Mohla there were two hand pumps thirty years ago, in 1949 there were thirteen, and in 1955 there were thirty-three. The blacksmith nowadays installs and repairs them. When Petromax lamps and sewing machines were introduced, he also learned to repair these. With the installment of diesel engines, some blacksmiths have learned to run and repair them. Others have opened hardware stores in the cities. Some educate their sons, but if possible they retain them in the same craft.

The cobbler used to make harnesses and eye shades for buffaloes, belts for churning pots, and leather *hukas,* but his main work was to sew and repair the native shoes for his *seypis.* But nowadays people want machine-made shoes in the city styles. Some village cobblers have learned to sew shoes on machines in the cities. A cobbler in Dhirke has installed a machine in his village and makes the new style loafers for men and high-heeled shoes for women, for which he has many customers in the neighboring villages. However, he continues to make native shoes, for which there is still much demand. A few cobblers have begun to deal in hides.

Unlike some of the other *kammis,* the village tailor is busier than ever before. Formerly, he combined the work of tailoring and laundering, but nowadays he is either a tailor or a washerman. People want more clothes and, with machine-made cloth and sewing machines, they can have them. By working all the time, the one tailor family in Mohla—husband and wife—can barely keep up with the work in Mohla and one other village. In one day the tailor can finish three complete outfits. If the family of the *chowdhri* or some other well-to-do *zamindar* wants city-made clothes, the tailor arranges to have a relative or friend in the city make the clothes as required.

The tailor in Mohla has four sons. Three go to school, but the youngest, who has no inclination for studies, takes care of the family buffalo. The oldest son, who will soon graduate from high school, may later do business in cloth. That is, he will buy cloth in the city and take it on a bicycle to sell in villages within a radius of twenty miles. The second son has great aptitude for sewing;

after he has finished high school and has worked for some tailor in the city, he intends to become a tailor like his father.

All these craftsmen, whose lives have long been affected by innovations, have adapted themselves to changing conditions but have remained in their traditional crafts. The details but not the over-all definitions of their occupations have been altered.

Others have had to adapt themselves in more diversified ways. The baker, who before the use of hand pumps supplied the houses with water, also collected fuel for the oven. His wife baked bread and parched grain. He himself was essentially a fisherman and a hunter of small game. This is still his main occupation, but he supplies the city market rather than selling fish or game in the villages. Also, since he is familiar with the river, he finds work as a ferryman or may be employed in connection with the water survey. There are six baker families in Mohla. The sons of one family are being educated; one son commutes daily on a bicycle to the city where he attends high school.

The *musallis,* who helped the farmer to cultivate the fields and did all kinds of unskilled labor, now also work on constructions, on the roads, and in factories. One *musalli* family is tenant on the land. Its oldest son is in the military but has his wife living in the village with his parents; the other three sons work on the land with their father. Another *musalli,* the head of a family, is a sweet maker who commutes on a bicycle to the city, where he sells the sweets he has made at home. Another *musalli* family makes straw mats which it sells in the village.

Thus, these craftsmen, whose occupations were somewhat diversified in the past, have adapted themselves to change by taking on other kinds of work—some of it familiar from the past, some of it new, some of it removing them from the village, or further from the village, during their working time, but without bringing about a severance of village ties or even, usually, of village residence.

It may be said that while village life remained very stable in terms of the people's point of view, interpersonal relations, and major preoccupations, over a long period the villagers have gradually adapted themselves to the use of technical innovations and have slowly modified their activities in so far as this was necessary or seemed to them desirable. Their outlook was conservative, and even insistent urging did not necessarily affect them. So, for instance, when Mohla was badly damaged by floods in 1950, the villagers—despite pleas by the more progressive of the *zamindars*—rebuilt the village just as it had been before.[1]

But with independence a whole series of possibilities for change opened up to the villagers as to all others in Pakistan. With the departure of the British, the Hindus, and the Sikhs, key posts were left open and business and trade came almost to a standstill. People were needed everywhere, and there was activity everywhere. The opening of schools in the villages, the political campaigns, the new right of men and women to vote, rural electrification, the introduction of the radio with special programs for villages, the installation of flour mills and of tube wells, the construction and improvement of roads, plans for village development programs—all these things and many others began to have their effect on village life and could be felt in Mohla.

One of the first and major jolts to traditional life was brought about by the enforcement of the Shariat Law of Inheritance, which gave women full rights of inheritance and applied to all families in which the father died after March 1948. In a few cases, daughters took advantage of the new laws and, although they had been married for years and had received their dowries—jewelry, clothes, bedding, furniture, utensils, buffaloes, and money—and during the years of their marriage had received presents from their *peke* on all big occasions, they now wanted their share in land as well. A

---

[1] Comparison of a detailed map of Mohla made in 1950 (before a devastating flood) with one made in 1952 (after the flood) indicates that in rebuilding the villagers reconstructed the old village exactly.

few cases were brought to court, but the brothers of these women tried to show that their sisters had in reality already received more than their share in their fathers' property. Such cases were handled with great caution and tact, so as to respect both the new law and the feelings of the people. Usually attempts were made to bring the parties to an understanding.

But such cases were few in number, and it was felt that they came up when the relationship between a brother and a sister was already strained, so that the new law provided them with an opportunity for bringing trouble into the open. Otherwise such cases would not come to court and sisters would not claim their property. In contrast, there were cases in which sisters transferred their property to their brothers by declaring that they had sold the land to them and had received the money. In this way, the claims of women who had married before the enforcement of the law were settled.

Nevertheless, *zamindars* and others who owned property became wary and began to transfer their property to their sons during their lifetime. So, for example, N.A., a *zamindar* in Gudyala village, who had three sons and three married daughters, in 1953 transferred his land to his sons, leaving only a small portion of the land for his wife, the income of which she could use for *nanekwali*, the portion of the dowry for the daughters' daughters. Though it was an expensive procedure, he preferred to undertake the expense rather than expose his sons to whatever inconveniences might be caused by his daughters or sons-in-law. He died in 1954, and, because two of his sons-in-law who were brothers had been troublesome all along and were not on good terms with their family-in-law, everybody now praised him for his wisdom and foresight.[2]

In cases where the father transfers the property to the sons, if he has an unmarried daughter he will make special provision for her or the brothers will take joint responsibility. Other ways of circumventing the law have also been found. For example, G.R., a small

---

[2] This kind of circumvention of the law takes place in cities also. So, for instance, the owner of a big city factory made his sons partners in his business.

zamindar of Mohla gave his daughter in marriage in exchange for a birde for his son. This was *vaṭo saṭa,* brother-sister exchange, a common form of marriage but one not very highly regarded. It was felt that in this case neither daughter would claim the right of inheritance, especially as both families are of the same status and their shares would be more or less equal. In looking for a match for their daughters, parents now try to make a connection with a family who will not claim land or other property and who will come to an understanding in advance that such claims will not be made. On the whole, this is not difficult because the number of women in the Punjab is smaller than that of men, particularly among poorer people. Also, in arranging a marriage, parents are more eager to make a good connection and to establish a good relationship with the other family than to get hold of property and, by so doing, to cut off the relationship. They know that the family of a girl will give her a dowry and afterwards will give her presents throughout her lifetime—because this is a matter of their own prestige as well as of the girl's prestige.

At present women themselves prefer not to risk destroying good relationships with their parental household. To ask for their share of inheritance from their brothers would go entirely against the love which a woman traditionally cherishes for her brother and against the picture of a respected and much loved *phuphi.* To do so would mean that she no longer had a *peke* to visit, who would give her the gifts that enhance her prestige, and who would be the first to share in her joys and sorrows. So, for example, the wife of Z.U. of the village of Talwandi, in the district of Gujranwala, and her two sisters—one of them a widow—inherited some land. They had no brother. But rather than each taking her share and allowing her husband to profit from it, they decided among themselves to transfer the land to the son of the widowed sister. These women wanted to have a *peke* where they could go to stay and to receive presents on proper occasions and thus gain *izzet,* prestige. By giving their land to their sister's son, they placed on him the responsibility of keeping up the tradition of the parental household.[3]

But a woman wishes to be on good terms with her paternal household for her husband's sake as well. For if her husband goes into politics or business, it is important for him to have a wide circle of connections, so he must maintain a good relationship not only with his own *biraderi* but also with his wife's relatives.

Thus, the initial response of those villagers who owned land, the *zamindars*, to the new laws supporting the equality of rights of men and women in the matter of inheritance was one of uneasiness; by new means they attempted to maintain the old equilibrium in which men were the holders of productive property and women shared in it through gifts which were their right, and in which both, through a good relationship expressed in giving and receiving, shared in the resulting prestige. In the new situation, where family relationships were good, the women supported the men.

For the *kammis* the right of equality as proclaimed in the Basic Principles[4] also had a great significance, since it meant that they could now buy land—no longer was the right of purchase restricted to the one caste. Up to now only a very few could avail themselves of this right, but it has given hope to all and has brought them satisfaction because now their desire for land can be fulfilled. With new opportunities to earn and to educate their children, they believe that they will also be able to buy land.

On the other hand, with regard to the inheritance laws—which met with an adverse reaction among the *zamindars* and others who owned property—the *kammis* have reacted in much the same way. For the *kammis* have also recognized the right of the daughter in her father's house and, according to their means, have given their daughters dowries and later have given them gifts on important

[3] In this instance the sisters followed the customary pattern according to which, lacking a male heir, land passed through a daughter to a daughter's son. (See discussion of *nanki virsa*, Chapter IV.)

[4] See Prologue.

occasions. It was for them no less than for the *zamindars* a source of pride and prestige to give to their own daughters and to the daughters of the house, for they practiced *vartan bhanji* in the same way, and it was just as important to them to gain prestige, power, and influence among their *biraderi*. It was their honor, and they would say, "I would rather let my life go but not my honor." So even though the new laws of inheritance would apply to them only in the future when they acquire land and property, the *kammis* felt as strongly as the *zamindars* did against giving a share of the inheritance to daughters and in this way disrupting the pattern of relationships from which their prestige derives.

Under the impact of the new laws, the *zamindar* felt that the value attached to land was undermined, that the power which was his through his ownership of the land was slipping away from him. But even in this bewildering situation, some men have begun to realize that although the land was the base on which one built the structure of ambition, there are now other possible bases on which a man can build to gain a more abundant income and to obtain prestige, influence, and power. The *zamindars,* as they had already begun to do, are moving beyond the villages to the cities and to other provinces wherever they can invest money, do business, or enter public life. However, usually their families remain in the villages. Whatever the men earn in money or gain in prestige and power, this does not make them want to leave the villages. On the contrary, they want to build a better life in the village.

A *zamindar* chooses his field of action according to his social and economic status. A big *zamindar,* who has 300 to 600 acres or more of arable land, invests money in business or industry or goes into political life. Most of the *zamindars* are modernizing agricultural techniques used on their land by introducing tractors and installing tube wells. These big *zamindars* were in politics before, but not in business.

A *zamindar,* who owns 100 to 300 acres of land, ventures into smaller businesses and looks forward to preparing his children for change through modern education.

Formerly, many well-to-do *zamindars* sent their sons to school, but if a boy did not show much eagerness to study the parents did not insist because the land was always there. Today both sons and daughters are being educated. The demand for educated girls has become widespread, and in the villages people have already learned to inquire whether a marriageable girl has completed primary or high school. In fact, as people are coming to prefer for a daughter-in-law an educated girl with a small dowry to an uneducated girl with a large dowry, parents are becoming eager to educate their daughters.

The *kammis* are equally eager to educate their children. Most of them send their children to the village school opened by the government, but not all of them as yet send their daughters to the same school with their sons. Instead, they still prefer to have their daughters study the Koran, which is taught by the wife of the *imam*. However, among the young men who have had some education, there is a strong desire to marry an educated girl who has studied in a regular school. So, for instance, a village blacksmith's son, who had attended high school, did not want to marry the girl to whom his parents had engaged him in childhood. He wanted a girl with education, but his parents would not listen. They went ahead with the marriage preparations and sent him off as a bridegroom with the *barat* to fetch the bride. At the girl's village, when the *nikah*—the reading of the marriage contract—was to be performed, the bridegroom refused to give his consent and, to the great humiliation of both sides, the *barat* returned without the bride. The marriage did not take place.

So, in various ways, both *zamindars* and *kammis* have been brought face to face with new problems and have tried to adapt themselves to new ways, or, on the contrary, they have tried to find new means of maintaining traditional ways. This can be seen not only in the attempts to circumvent the inheritance laws, but also in the demand for educated brides to marry educated bridegrooms where, to the old preferences for likeness in status and age and comeliness, likeness in education has been added.

In this new situation in the villages, both *zamindars* and *kammis* have seen and taken advantage of new opportunities and both have realized the importance of education. Formerly, the interest of both was centered on the land. The *zamindars* wanted more land and the *kammis* had an unquenchable thirst to own some land, and each group depended on the other to make the land produce and support all of them. But with new opportunities, it seemed possible that their interests might well diverge and that their old relationships—built up through work and responsibility, through services each rendered the other, and expressed in *vartan bhanji*—might break down.

In fact, in trying out new kinds of activities they have sought and found security and reassurance in mutual support. This may take many forms. For instance, a *zamindar* of the village of Samañ and a well-to-do *kammi* of the nearby village of Ghazi Chak have together opened a cloth shop in the village of Shadiwal, three miles away. And in the village of Dhirke, a carpenter has installed a flour mill and two *zamindars* have become his partners. Similarly, a *zamindar* who goes into politics and wants to run for election first calls together the *zamindars* and *kammis* of his own village and consults them about whether he should enter the election and whether they will support him and use their influence to get support from their friends and relatives. Only with their cooperation will he go ahead.

For a *kammi* it is a big step to send his son to the secondary school, and a man will ask for the advice and encouragement of a *zamindar* before doing so. Together they will discuss the prospects of work for the boy, and the *zamindar* will promise his support. If his son is already through the secondary school, the *kammi*—or for that matter the less influential *zamindar*—will seek the help of an influential *zamindar* to recommend a boy for some job or will ask his advice about whether the boy should go to a technical school, enter college, or join the military. But there are also situations in which a *zamindar* may ask for the advice of a *kammi*. Babu Imam-Din, of the village of Samañ, who is in his fifties and is a barber by caste, has a high school education and for years has been employed as a clerk in the railway engineering department. For this reason, the *zamindars* of his own and of a neighboring village often come to ask his advice about educating their sons and about the prospects of jobs.

In the village of Mohla there are twelve boys who commute daily to the city of Gujrat by bicycle. Two go to college and ten to the high school; four are *zamindar* boys and eight are *kammis*.[5] The son of the weaver in Mohla has finished the secondary school and, on the advice of the *chowdhri*, has joined the military.

In the same way, *kammis* who have educated sons are likely to ask the help of *zamindars* when they want to arrange a son's marriage. In the village of Khaiderabad, in the district of Lyallpur, the son of a former tenant of H.S. finished the secondary school, joined the military, and is now a captain. His parents wanted to arrange a marriage for the young man. They had a connection in the city with a family of their own weaver caste who had an educated daughter. However, they felt that they did not have much experience outside the village and consequently might not be sufficiently discriminating in their choice of a city girl for their son. So they turned for advice and help to H.S. He is a rather poor landowner who owned about fifteen acres of land, but to these *kammis* he appears to be a worldly man because he has traveled widely in the province to attend religious conferences held in Lahore or Multan or Gujrat, because he has many connections, and because he has performed *Haj* twice—such a man should know. H.S. was very willing to help. He went to the city with the father of the young man, met the family of the girl, saw the girl herself, and approved. Thereafter the marriage was arranged to everyone's satisfaction.

[5] In Mohla, the ratio of *zamindars* to *kammis* is one to three.

This tenant family had previously worked for H.S. Now their status has been raised because their son is a military officer and they are well off. Yet the fact of their higher status has not affected their relationship to H.S. On the contrary, they feel that in their present position they are in greater need of guidance and advice from a person like H.S. than they would have been in their former position. Indeed, had their son been uneducated, they would not have consulted H.S. before arranging his marriage. But now the fact that they have asked help from H.S. and that he has given it makes for a closer relationship between them, and this relationship extends to their son and daughter-in-law as well, for they were married through the mediation of H.S.

So far, the pattern of village life has not been disrupted by change. Whatever new is to be learned in the cities, the village people are willing—even eager—to learn, but they bring their newly acquired knowledge and techniques back to the village. They are not uprooted. A *zamindar* goes into business and may be away for months, but his family remains in the village and he returns there. A *kammi* may work outside the village, but he maintains his house in the village. No matter how much a man may improve his knowledge or earn elsewhere, outside his village he does not get personal satisfaction; for him, his *biraderi* and his village are the framework within which he measures his success.

And yet, no matter how little the villages have actually been affected by change, the desire for change extends to the village itself. That is, just as people have a deep desire to improve their own lot, so too they have a deep desire to improve the village. There are some indications that this may be done on some sort of communal basis. For instance, on the advice of more enlightened *zamindars* and some wise *kammis*, village people have begun to cut down the expenses of marriage and circumcision by eliminating some of the ceremonies and have given the money so saved to a village fund. Thus, at a marriage, a *zamindar* family will give from 50 to 100 rupees, and a *kammi* family from 30 to 40 rupees to the

new community fund. (Within this range, the amount contributed
at the marriage of a boy is larger than that contributed at the marriage of a girl.) Similarly, on the occasion of circumcision, a *zamindar* family will give 30 rupees, and a *kammi* family 20 rupees.
A poor *kammi* need not make a contribution when his son is circumcised because, customarily, his child is circumcised together
with the child of a well-to-do *zamindar* or *kammi*. But even if the
poor *kammi* has this ceremony performed at his own home he need
not contribute.

Although initially there were many who approved of this plan,
there were even more who objected to it. They felt they could not
swallow their pride. They asked: "What are they going to do with
their nose?" (The nose is the symbol of honor.) Those who now
wanted to contribute to the community fund had in the past accepted food and sweets on occasions when people had celebrated
marriages or circumcisions. "Will they not reciprocate now?" people asked. "Who will believe or remember that a marriage was
properly performed unless food and sweets are distributed in the
village?" The idea that the customs with which they had grown up
and according to which they had arranged their lives would be replaced by new ways made them feel very insecure. They needed
reassurance. This they obtained when it was said that the new ways
put no restrictions on them. Whoever wished to distribute food and
sweets was free to do so; only the family must contribute to the
village fund as well.

In connection with cutting down the expenses of a marriage,
some ceremonies have been discontinued and others have been
shortened. Formerly the ceremonies extended over a period of
about a month, from the celebration of the *gala* to the time when
the *barat*, the wedding procession, went to the bride's home and
brought her back to the bridegroom's home.

Actually, as it has been pointed out, the ceremonies connected
with marriage may be divided into two parts. The first part begins
with the *gala* and ends with the *meyl*, the gathering of the wedding

guests. The ceremonies that take place both in the bridegroom's village and in the bride's village within this period are the ones in which most or all of the village people participate. The second part of the ceremonies begins with the arrival of the *meylis,* the wedding guests, and continues until after the departure of the *barat* from the bridegroom's village (for the family of the bridegroom) and from the bride's village (for the family of the bride). The *meylis* who take part in the second part of the ceremonies are the *biraderi,* the relatives and the close friends of the respective families celebrating the event.

Vartan bhanji was the main feature of both of these sets of ceremonies. To the village people, the house of marriage distributed food and sweets, and the village people brought wheat and gave money to be given to the *kammis* of the house where the marriage was being celebrated. With the *meylis, vartan bhanji* was carried on much more intensively with sweets, food, yard goods for *jowṛas,* and money.

Nowadays, in many villages, the marriage ceremonies begin with the *maiyañ,* the ceremony in which a bracelet of colored thread is tied around the wrist of the bride or bridegroom; this takes place a few days before the *barat.*[6] The ceremonies of *gala, sambhal,* and *vaṛ* are now omitted.[7] In such cases, the *maiyañ* also is much simplified, as only a small quantity of wheat (around sixteen pounds) is cooked and distributed among the visitors, the village women and children; here the giving of food is no more than a token. This means that, on the whole, the distribution of food and sweets in the village, as it formerly took place on such occasions, has been discontinued. However, the other main feature of the *maiyañ*— namely, the sending of cooked meals by members of the *biraderi* to

---

[6] However, there are exceptions. There are parents who have an only son and whose great desire is to perform all the ceremonies.

[7] For descriptions of these various ceremonies, see especially Chapter XVI *passim,* in which are described, in connection with the articles used in *vartan bhanji* at a wedding, the occasions on which gifts are given and distributions are made.

the house of marriage, which is part of their *vartan bhanji* relationship—has been continued.

The distributions of sweets and food in the village, which were
part of *vartan bhanji* with the village as a whole, served the purpose of unifying all the people in the village—making them feel
that they all were participating in the event and that everyone belonged to the same community. In the eyes of those who have accepted the plan for discontinuing the distributions to the village in
the wedding ceremonies preliminary to the *maiyañ* and for giving
money to the community fund instead, the contributions to the
fund serve a like purpose. The money collected is used to pave the
streets or to build a mosque or a village school, and the village
people feel that there is a common bond and a common source of
pride in the improved village.

At the same time, it is noteworthy that the distribution of sweets
customarily made when the bride first comes to the village of her
parents-in-law and on the occasions of her successive visits to her
parents and her parents-in-law—as well as on lesser occasions—
continue as before. These serve the double purpose of uniting the
village and of emphasizing the girl's relationship to the two villages
—to her own village as a daughter of a house whose rights continue after her marriage, and to the village of her parents-in-law
as a daughter-in-law, who will develop her own set of relationships
to the villagers.

Returning to the second part of the marriage ceremonies, certain
changes have also taken place in these. For example, the length of
the stay of the *barat* in the bride's village has been shortened.
Formerly, the *barat* stayed for at least one night. Now the *barat*
comes and leaves on the same day. At first some people were highly
critical of the new way, but eventually most people found it very
practical. However, such changes as have taken place have not
affected the *vartan bhanji* with the *meylis;* food, money, cloth, and
quantities of sweets are exchanged as before. As this part of the
ceremonies has remained unchanged and as *vartan bhanji* is carried

on as usual, the daughter—who receives the customary gifts from her father's house—remains the key figure together with the "daughters of the house," who also receive.

In the past, villages were bound together by many complex relationships. These took a variety of forms. Some villages were bound to each other through intermarriage; some had a common boundary; some were founded by a group of brothers or by a brother and a sister; one might be an offshoot of another. There are villages where people of the same subcaste live; villages which belong to the same district administrative unit, and so, for instance, share a police station; and neighboring villages may share the services of certain *kammis*—carpenter, blacksmith, weaver, tailor, washerman, or butcher. Several villages may feel bound to one in which there lives a *pir*, or to one which has a market used by all of them.

The women married in Mohla come from the surrounding villages and from others farther away. For these women, the villages from which they come are their *peke;* for their children the same villages are their *nanke;* for their husbands they are their *saure.* In turn, the people of Mohla have connections and feel strong bonds of relationship with the villages where their sisters and daughters and daughters' daughters are married. The villages founded long ago by a group of brothers feel related and this relationship is celebrated by the village bards who know the genealogies. And the villages in which live numerous *zamindars* of the same subcaste also feel related.

These relationships have been the basis of a great deal of inter-village feeling and activity. As has been described, there was between two such villages buying for cash or on credit, lending, visiting to attend a joyful occasion such as a marriage, to offer condolences at a time of sorrow, or to take part in religious gatherings, or to carry on the work of the *parea* (the village council), and there was also extensive exchange of favors, as in asking for *mang* (collective labor). Whatever the original connection between two villages may have been, it was elaborated over time into a whole complex of relationships that made the villages interdependent.

In the new situation, new types of connections have been added to the older ones. Some of the *zamindars* and some of the *kammis* in different villages have entered into business partnerships. The people of their own and of neighboring villages have become their clients, and this has made for more relationships between the villages. In politics, certain villages have been grouped together as one voting constituency. Within each constituency various alliances have been formed to back candidates; these, too, have drawn villages together. Each of the schools opened by the government is another focus of common interest as children from several villages attend the school located in one of them. The villages are, furthermore, jointly responsible for the construction of the school building, which again gives all of them a basis for cooperation since, to have a school, they must be willing to share in building it.

Thus, although the village people are now in the midst of change, it would appear that they are able to deal with the sudden multiplicity of new possibilities much as in the past they were able to deal with the innovations which—often as isolated bits—came into the villages more slowly from the larger world. Their initial responses to the new indicate that neither the pattern of village life nor the emphasis upon good relationships has been deeply affected.

Seyp: Work and Payments

A *seyp* is a work relationship between a *zamindar* and a *kammi* or between two *kammis* through which they share mutual obligations for work and payment. Every household has a group of *kammis,* the *kammis* of the house, each of whom works for that house, carrying on his craft and the tasks related to it and also, in the case of *seyp* between *zamindar* and *kammi,* working on the land. The relationship between *seypis,* those who have a *seyp,* has been discussed in Chapter III, on the village castes.

Table 1, below, indicates the nature of the craft work done by seven different craftsmen (and their wives or mothers), the members of seven different castes: the barber, the blacksmith, the carpenter, the cobbler, the potter, the baker, and the *musalli,* or agricultural laborer. It indicates the occasions on which each one receives payment for work done in the course of one year and the types of payment made on those occasions by a *seypi* who is a *zamindar* by caste and by one who is a *kammi.*

In general, the *zamindar* makes these customary payments irrespective of the amount of work done by the particular *kammi* during the year. *Kammis* make payments only for work which actually is done; however, *kammis* do owe their *kammis* of the house *laag,* the money which is given only on the occasion of a marriage, a birth, a circumcision, or the death of an elderly person in the household of the donor.

TABLE 1. SEYP: ANNUAL WORK UNITS FOR KAMMIS OF HOUSE AND ANNUAL PAYMENTS MADE BY ZAMINDARS AND BY KAMMIS

Work and Payments	Barber	Blacksmith	Carpenter	Cobbler
Unit of Work for Each Seypi	Haircuts for 1 man and 2–6 children	Work on one plough	Work on one plough	Making 4 pairs of shoes, repairing shoes, etc.
Number of Seypis	15–30	15–30	15–30	15–30
Payment by Zamindar				
Summer harvest				
wheat (lbs.)	40	40	40	40
straw (lbs.)	80	80	80	80
fodder (lbs.)	80–100, once or twice in season	80–100, once or twice in season	80–100, once or twice in season	80–100, once or twice in season
Autumn harvest				
rice or maize (lbs.)	30	30	30	30
sugarcane (canes)	50–60	50–60	50–60	50–60
fodder	As in summer harvest	As in summer harvest	As in summer harvest	As in summer harvest
Meals	For cooking at ceremony, meal for family[a]; for errand, meal for self; on 3 Ids, meal for family	At ceremonies, meal for family; for work on well, meal for self; on 3 Ids, meal for family	At ceremonies, meal for family; for repair work, meal for self; on 3 Ids, meal for family	At ceremonies, meal for family; on 3 Ids, meal for family
Laag[b]				
marriage (rupees)	25–35; 15–25	5–10; 3–5	5–10; 2–3	50–75; 40–50[c]
birth, circumcision (rupees)	10–15; 5–10	2–3; 1–2	2–3; 1–2	2–3; 1–2
death of elderly person (rupees)	5–10; 3–5	2–3; 1–2	2–3; 1–2	2–3; 1–2
Miscellaneous		For taking care of well for one group of 2 to 6 partners, 150 lbs. wheat	If well has wood- (not iron-) work, 150 lbs. wheat	For making eyeshades for oxen, extra grain
Payments by Kammis				
Annual	25 lbs. wheat	Payment in money or grain, according to work done	Payment in money or grain, according to work done	Payment in money or grain, according to work done
Laag[b]				
marriage (rupees)	15–20; 10–15	3–5; 2–3	3–5; 2–3	3–5; 2–3
birth, circumcision (rupees)	5–10; 3–5	2–3; 1	2–3; 1	2–3; 1
death of elderly person (rupees)	5–8; 3–5	2–3; 1	2–3; 1	2–3; 1

TABLE 1.—Continued

Work and Payments Unit of Work for Each Seypi	Potter	Baker	Laborer (Musalli)
	20-30 household wares bought twice a year by well-to-do; others buy fewer, pay by number	Wife does daily baking for family	Woman cleans house and court; makes dung cakes from dung of 6 to 8 cattle[d] Man works in fields[d]
Number of Seypis	25-50	20-30	4-6 households (for both man and woman)
Payment by Zamindar			
Summer harvest			
wheat (lbs.)	160	16-20	300
straw (lbs.)	80	80	80
fodder (lbs.)	80-100, once or twice in season	80-100, once or twice in season	80-100, once or twice in season
Autumn harvest			
rice or maize (lbs.)	100	16-20	150
sugarcane (canes)	50-60	20-30	50-60
fodder	As in summer harvest	As in summer harvest	As in summer harvest
Meals	At ceremonies, meal for family; carrying grain to mill, meal for self; on 3 Ids, meal for family	At ceremonies, meal for family; for errand, meal for self; on 3 Ids, meal for family	At ceremonies, meal for family, meal for self; on 3 Ids, meal for family
Laag[b]			
marriage (rupees)	5-10; 3-5	5-10; 3-5	5-10; 3-5
birth, circumcision (rupees)	2-3; 1-2	2-3; 1-2	2-3; 1-2
death of elderly person (rupees)	2-3; 1-2	2-3; 1-2	2-3; 1-2
Miscellaneous	Collects dung twice a year from houses of seypis	Paid daily, 1 bread for each 8 baked; paid 8-12 lbs. grain for each delivery of fish	
Payments by Kammis			
Annual	Payment is money or grain, according to wares bought	Paid daily, 1 bread for each 8 baked; fish paid for in grain or money	None; receives laag and meals only
Laag[b]			
marriage (rupees)	3-5; 2-3	3-5; 2-3	3-5; 2-3
birth, circumcision (rupees)	2-3; 1	2-3; 1	2-3; 1
death of elderly person (rupees)	2-3; 1	2-3; 1	2-3; 1

[a] Meal for family is for six persons.
[b] Figures show range of laag payment by well-to-do and by less well-to-do.
[c] Payment made to cobbler at marriage depends on number and quality of pairs of shoes made; if there is much gold work on shoes he will receive a buffalo or a payment of more than 100 rupees.
[d] For some zamindars, woman sweeps only on ceremonial days and man works in fields for only 2 or 3 days in year. For kammis, woman sweeps only on ceremonial days.

The Farmer's Round of Activities

The middle of April is the beginning of the year for the farmer. This is the month of *Bisakh*. At this time, the "thirteenth month," the period of hardship is coming to an end and the period of plenitude is approaching because the major crops are standing in the fields and the farmer knows that somewhere in the Punjab—depending upon the climate—the harvest has started on the first day of *Bisakh*. To celebrate the first day of *Bisakh*, a country fair, *Bisakhi*, formerly was held throughout the province, but after partition it was discontinued as a Hindu custom. Nevertheless, the farmer is fully aware of the first day of *Bisakh*, for to him it means the beginning of harvest. He watches the weather on that day as it is of special significance to him. If the first part of the day is clear and calm, the vegetables and tobacco—which he planted at the end of the year and which are in blossom now—will grow in abundance; but if the morning is stormy, then the crop will not be abundant or may fail.

Table 2, below, outlines the farmer's allocation of time in the course of one year, which was discussed in some detail in Chapter V. It shows also the Punjabi months, which follow the Gregorian calendar. The dates given are approximations, first because there is some annual variation in rainfall, and therefore in the dates when the crops are ready, and second because there are local variations from one part of the Punjab to another, due to slight climatic variations and differences in the mode of irrigation. In Mohla, the "thirteenth month" continues into *Bisakh*, which is also the first month of the farming calendar.

TABLE 2. THE FARMER'S ROUND OF ACTIVITIES

Punjabi Months*	Farmer's Seasons	Seasonal Activities
Bisakh	End thirteenth month (to April 21) Good food scarcity.	
——— Jeth	Summer harvest and planting (April 22–June 7)	Very intensive work. Cutting of maize, millet for fodder, wheat (main crop of year); payment of house kammis and others. Planting of cotton, fodder, millet, maize. Dry weather; frequent irrigation.
Har	Leisure, marriages (June 8–July 8)	Little work, plentiful food. Season of country fairs, marriages. Cutting of tobacco just before rains begin.
Sawan	Monsoon rains (July 9–Aug. 14)	Period of anxiety: hope and fear because of rains. With first rains, planting of paddy begins. Irrigation if rains delayed.
Bhaduñ	Waiting (Aug. 15–Sept. 14)	Very little work besides care of cattle, ploughing of fallow fields, weeding paddy.
Asuj ——— Katak	Autumn harvest and planting (Sept. 15–Nov. 30)	Period of very intensive work. As soon as fields dry after rains, commence ploughing. Harvesting of millet, maize, rice. Planting of autumn crops of wheat, barley, gram, lentils, fodder, chilies.
Maghar ——— Poh ——— Magh	Winter, marriages (Dec. 1–Feb. 28)	Period of little work on land, except care of cattle, cutting fodder, weeding crops. With rain, fodder abundant; otherwise scarce. After rains, ploughing of fields for spring planting. Picking of cotton, chilies; cutting of sugarcane begins and continues into next period. (Main period of craft activities in village.)
Phagan	Spring planting (March 1–31)	Moderately hard work. Planting of tobacco, sugarcane, maize and millet for fodder, vegetables.
Chet	Thirteenth month	Little work except care of cattle and harvesting of lentils, gram, barley.

* Months follow Gregorian calendar.

Vehi: The Family Register

Every family has a family register, *vehi,* which may be kept for generations. In this register are recorded the sums of money which are received from other families and the sums of money given to other families as *neondra* at a wedding or on the occasion of *roti,* an invitation to a meal at the death of an old person. The money given to a *kammi* as *vedaigi,* in connection with a wedding celebration, is also recorded.

A single entry system of bookkeeping is customary. The book is started from both ends simultaneously. The money received is entered at one end, and that given is entered at the other end. All the sums of money given or received on any one occasion are entered together.

In fact, most families keep a record only of the sums of money they have received—with the name of each individual and the amount given by him recorded—and depend upon the records of the people with whom they deal and upon their own memory for information about the money they have given. The register is in the keeping of the women of the family, who may not be able to read but who know its contents by heart.

Table 3, below, is a reproduction of one page from the *vehi* of a *kammi* family in Mohla, a partial record of *neondra* received on the occasion of the marriage of a son of the house. In all, 55 male wedding guests contributed money, and 209 rupees were collected. This marriage took place in 1909, when money had comparatively greater value than at present. Nowadays, depending upon the family's status, money collected as *neondra* ranges from a few hundred to a few thousand rupees.

TABLE 3. A PAGE FROM A FAMILY REGISTER

Memorandum of the money received on the occasion of marriage of Rahmat, son of Fathe Din, baker of Mohla

15. 8. 1909

From our own house				Rs.	1
K.M.	*baker	[of]	Mohla		15
M.J.	*chowdhri*		Mohla		2
I.B.	*baker		Mohla		9
A.D.	carpenter		Mohla		1
M.D.†	foreman		Khanke		2
F.D.	baker		Khanke		21
L.	baker		Rana		8
W.	baker		Koulowala		1
P.M.	*baker		Mohla		4
I. Singh‡			Mohla		7
M.C.	*chowdhri*		Mohla		2
A.Y.	*chowdhri*		Mohla		2
R.	weaver		Mohla		1
F.D.	bard		Mohla		2
A.D.	barber		Mohla		1
J.	Kashmiri		Mohla		1
G.M.	laborer		Mohla		1
K.D.	*baker		Jendiala		2
N.D.	baker		Kot Nathu		1
N.K.	baker		Wazirabad		1
O.B.	baker		Lundpur		8 with *khara*

* *Biraderis* of the family; other bakers are relatives.

† The foreman was a friend whose subcaste was not recorded.

‡ I. Singh, a Sikh, was a shopkeeper in Mohla who left the village in 1930. Because he lived in Mohla he was regarded as *biraderi* (in the extended meaning of term). *Chowdhri* is used to refer to *zamindars* in general; they are regarded as *biraderis* in the same sense as I. Singh.

Intermarriage among Kin

Marriage within the kin group is the most favored form of marriage. In connection with marriage, people would say: "A half from one's own home is better than a whole from outside." In other words, it is better to marry one's sons and daughters to relatives than to bring in outsiders. A man usually shows a strong desire to have his sister's daughter for a daughter-in-law, and a woman wishes her son to marry her brother's daughter. The usual pattern is for a girl to marry into the same family that her father's sister did. Parents, who arrange the marriages of their children, try to make suitable matches in terms of age, appearance, and —today—level of education of the prospective spouses. Only if there is no suitable match within the extended kin group do they look outside to make a marriage connection. Then, if this connection proves to be a satisfactory one, more marriages are likely to follow between the same two families.

The two accompanying charts, Figures 3 and 4, illustrate intermarriage within kin group. The time span covered by the charts is about one hundred years. Figure 3 shows the descendants of two brothers and a sister; the men and women who married outside the three resulting families are not shown. It seems that as long as there were suitable marriages, the descendants were married within these three families.

Figure 4 illustrates intermarriage within one family. On this chart, all the descendants are shown regardless of whether they married within or outside the family. The spouses of those who married outside the family are not indicated, but the children of males are shown. The family analyzed on this chart is the same family as Family I on the first chart.

These two charts indicate that while in the second and third generations almost all the girls were married within the kin group, in the fourth (the present) generation, even though there were suitable matches, the number of marriages to relatives has decreased. Figure 4 shows that in the present generation, there are 28 girls. Of these, 7 are married to relatives, and 9 to outsiders; the remaining 12 will most probably marry outside. Of the 19 boys, 8 are married to relatives, 4 to nonrelatives; of the remaining 7, 5 are of marriageable age and 2 are too young as yet. In this fourth generation, out of a total of 47 boys and girls, 15 are married to relatives and 13 are married to outsiders. Among

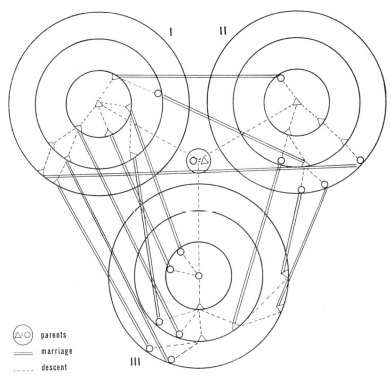

FIGURE 3. INTERMARRIAGE AMONG THREE FAMILIES

Each of the concentric circles represents one generation successively removed from the progenitors at the center. All of the people in each set of concentric circles are *biraderi*. All of the members of Family I and Family II are also *biraderi* because they are the descendants of two brothers. Family I and Family II are not *biraderi* of Family III, whose members are the descendants of a sister married into another *biraderi*.

the others, some are too young, but with regard to those who are of marriageable age, the parents are trying to find matches outside the kin group despite the fact that there are suitable matches within it.

Up to the present, marriages have been arranged by parents without consideration for individual preferences; indeed, such preferences have not been shown by the young people concerned. Yet there does seem to be some tendency, however slight, for families to form new connections outside the kin group.

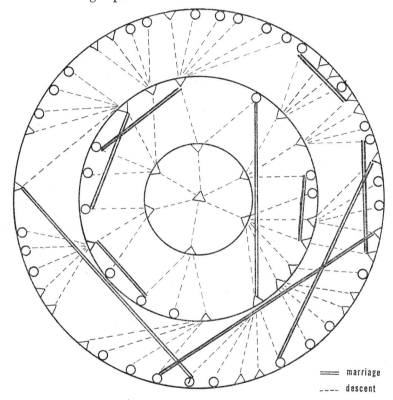

FIGURE 4. INTERMARRIAGE IN ONE FAMILY

Each of the concentric circles represents one generation successively removed from the progenitors at the center. The spouses of those who are not married within this family are not shown, but the descendants of males are shown.

Main Ceremonies Connected with Marriage

The ceremonies connected with a marriage cover a prolonged period of time, including both the period during which the families of the bride and of the bridegroom make the necessary formal preparations and the period of the actual marriage. During the preparatory period, ceremonies take place in the village of the bride's family and of the groom's family, respectively, and involve participation primarily of people living in that village. The later ceremonies, some of which take place in both villages, some in the village of the groom's family and some in the village of the bride's family, also involve participation of the invited wedding guests, the *meylis*, relatives and friends who may come from other places.

Many of the ceremonies for bride and groom parallel each other, though not all of them take place simultaneously. Thus, such ceremonies as *gala*, which opens the sequence, and *maiyañ*, when a knotted cord is tied to the wrist of the bride and of the groom, take place approximately at the same time in both villages. But the ceremonies of *khara lhai*, dressing, and of *selami*—bathing, dressing, and salutation of bride and of groom—take place at different times: for the groom, before he departs with the *barat*, the wedding party, for the bride's village; for the bride, later, before she departs with the groom and the wedding party for the groom's village.

Certain ceremonies are not customarily carried out by both families. *Vag pharai*, for example, the ceremony in which the groom's sisters and cousins hold onto the bridle of his horse until he presents them with money, has no parallel for the bride. *Var* and *sambhal* are performed customarily only by the family of the groom but in exceptional circumstances might be performed by the family of the bride. A few ceremonies, principally *thehan* and *ratha chari*, which are performed by men in the family of the groom in the village of the bride and which honor daughters and daughters-in-law of the groom's village, are optionally performed by the more well-to-do.

Table 4 outlines the main ceremonies connected with marriage which involve the giving and receiving of gifts and which are discussed in the body of this study in connection with the description of *vartan bhanji*. The chart gives the names of the ceremonies and indicates where they take place—in the boy's village or in the girl's village. It shows further the types of gifts given to the family and distributed by them as discussed in the text (food, sweets, money and valuables, and clothes), by whom and to whom they are given.

For the sake of convenience, the ceremonies have been numbered, indicating the general sequence. It should be borne in mind, however, that in some cases more than one ceremony may be taking place at approximately the same time. Thus, while the bridal party from the groom's family is in the bride's village, ceremonies such as *thehan* and *ratha chari* may be taking place in the men's guest house while, elsewhere, the groom is dressing in the outfit given him by the bride's family.

The chart indicates points at which *laag* is given to *kammis* (for example, 14 and 30); in fact, the giving of *laag* goes on at different stages of each ceremony. In this chart, no attempt has been made to include all the actual details, but only to provide, in outline form, a guide to the placement of the principal events.

TABLE 4. MAIN CEREMONIES AND GIFTS CONNECTED WITH MARRIAGE

Ceremonies and Category of Gifts	Groom's Side		Bride's Side	
	Gifts received[a]	Gifts distributed[b]	Gifts received[a]	Gifts distributed[b]
1. Gala				
food	from village: *veyl*	to house *kammis*: *veyl* in village: *gur*	from village: *veyl*	to house *kammis*: *veyl* in village: *gur*
sweets				
clothes	from mother's *peke*: *hath phareda*		from mother's *peke*: *hath phareda*, for mother of bride	
2. Maiyañ				
food	from village: *veyl* from *biraderis*: cooked meals	to house *kammis*: *veyl* to village: boiled wheat	from village: *veyl* from *biraderis*: cooked meals	to house *kammis*: *veyl* in village: boiled wheat
money, valuables				
clothes	from guests: *chowl*	to house *kammis*: *chowl* to women *kammis* of house: *jowras*	from guests: *chowl*	to house *kammis*: *chowl* to women *kammis* of house: *jowras*
3. Vaṭ				
food		in village: wheat, lentils		
4. Sambhal				
food		in village: cooked rice		

	Received	Given	Received	Given
5. *Ledu* sweets		in village: *ledu*		
6. *Mhendi* food	from village: *veyl*	to house *kammis*: *veyl* to guests: *henna*	from village: *veyl*	to house *kammis*: *veyl* to guests: *henna*
7. Arrival of Wedding Guests, *Meyli* food		to friends in village and neighboring villages: cooked meals	from friends in villages and neighboring villages: uncooked food from *nanke*: sweets	
sweets	from sister and father's sister: sweets			
money, valuables, clothes	from sister: gold ring for groom from sister and father's sister: *jowras*		from *nanke*: *nanekwali* (bedding, copperware, etc., gold ornaments, *jowras*) for bride	
8. Feast for *Meyli* food		to *meyli, kammis*: feast to those from whom food received: trays of food		(For corresponding ceremonies for bride, see below, ceremonies performed while wedding party, *barat*, is in village of bride.)

TABLE 4.—Continued

Ceremonies and Category of Gifts	Groom's Side		Bride's Side	
	Gifts received[a]	Gifts distributed[b]	Gifts received[a]	Gifts distributed[b]
			(For corresponding ceremonies for bride, see 27, below.)	
9. *Khara Lhai*				
money, valuables	mother's brother: money, buffalo or horse, for groom			
clothes		to *kammis* who assist in bath: old *lungi*, from groom		
10. (Dressing of Groom)				
money, valuables				
clothes	from father's sister: *jowra*, for groom; from *arain*: veil of flowers, for groom	to tailor, barber, *arain*: *laag*, from groom		
11. *Neondra*				
money, valuables	from male guests: money			
12. *Selami*				
money, valuables	from guests: money, for groom			

		From	To
13.	*Servarna* money, valuables	from women relatives: money	to house *kammis:* money
14.	*Laag* money, valuables		to house *kammis: laag*
15.	*Vag Pharai* money, valuables		to sister and female cousins: money, from groom
16.	Departure of Wedding Party, *Barat,* for Bride's Village, with *Varasui* (Clothes, Ornaments, *bid*) for Bride		
17.	Departure of *Meyli* from Groom's Home sweets		to wedding guests: sweets
	clothes		to wedding guests: *jowras*

TABLE 4.—Continued

Ceremonies and Category of Gifts	Groom's Side		Bride's Side	
	Gifts received[a]	*Gifts distributed*[b]	*Gifts received*[a]	*Gifts distributed*[b]
18. Arrival of *Barat* in Bride's Village				
19. *Nikah*, Reading of the Marriage Contract, in Bride's Village[c] money, valuables		to village *ínam* who performs *nikah:* money, from groom's father		
20. Feast for *Barati* food				to *barati, meyli, kammis:* wedding feast to those from whom food had been received: trays of food

21. *Thelan*
    sweets,
    money, val-
    uables

    from father of groom:
    gifts and sweets,
    for women from
    groom's village
    married into bride's
    village

22. Display of
    Bride's
    Dowry
    (Gifts Given
    by Bride's
    Nanke and
    by Her Par-
    ents)

23. Dressing of
    Groom[d]
    money, val-
    uables
    clothes

    from groom: money,
    for *kammis* of
    bride's house

24. *Ratha Chari*
    money, val-
    uables

    to groom: *jowra*; veil
    of flowers, to be
    donned by him

    to bards from villages
    whose daughters
    and daughters'
    daughters are mar-
    ried into groom's
    village: money,
    from groom's father

TABLE 4.—Continued

Ceremonies and Category of Gifts	Groom's Side		Bride's Side	
	Gifts received[a]	Gifts distributed[b]	Gifts received[a]	Gifts distributed[b]
25. *Chul* money, valuables			from father of groom: money, for *kammis* of bride's village	
26. Display of *Varasui*, Gifts Brought to Bride by Bridegroom				
27. *Khara Lhai* money, valuables, clothes	(For corresponding ceremonies for groom, see 9, above.)		from mother's brother: money, buffalo or horse, for bride	to both assistants: old *lungi*, from bride
28. Dressing of Bride money, valuables, clothes			from groom's family: clothes, ornaments, etc., to be donned by bride	to barber's wife: *laag*, from groom's father

No.	Ceremony	From	To
29.	*Selami* money, valuables,		
30.	*Laag* money, valuables		to *kammis* of bride's village: *laag*[9]
31.	Departure of *Barat* from Bride's Village with Bride, Groom, and Dowry	from *meyli:* money, for bride and groom	
32.	Departure of *Meyli* from Bride's Home sweets, money, valuables, clothes		to *meyli:* sweets to daughters of house and sons-in-law: sweets, money, *jowras*
33.	Return of *Barat* to Bridegroom's Village		

TABLE 4.—Continued

Ceremonies and Category of Gifts	Groom's Side		Bride's Side	
	Gifts received[a]	Gifts distributed[b]	Gifts received[a]	Gifts distributed[b]
34. *Selami* money, valuables		to bride: money, from groom's mother, sister, father's sister		
35. (Unnamed) food sweets			in village: *khichṛi* in village: *leḍus*	
36. Bride's *Muklava:* Departure of Groom's Sister, Father's Sister[c] sweets, money, valuables, clothes		from bride: *leḍus* to sisters, father's sisters: sweets; money or ornaments or horse or buffalo; *jowras*		

37. Bride's
Tarwianda[z]
food   in village: *khichri*
              (prepared by
               bride)

[a] Unless otherwise specified, gifts are received by the household of the bridegroom or of the bride.

[b] Unless otherwise specified, gifts are distributed by the household of the bridegroom or of the bride.

[c] This ceremony takes place inconspicuously and does not involve participation of wedding guests, *meyli.*

[d] Sequence of groom's dressing not fixed.

[e] Money to pay this *laag* may be offered by the groom's family, but usually is refused wholly or in part and is given by the bride's family.

[f] Bridegroom's father's sister and sister do not leave with other wedding guests, but remain with their *peke*, paternal relatives, until the bride comes to the village for her second visit.

[g] This distribution may take place at the time of the bride's third visit, or alternatively, when she settles down to live in the household of her parents-in-law.

Glossary

amaji	Mother; see also *bebeji*
ang	Daughters of a mirasi's village married into another village
*anna**	One-sixteenth of a rupee
apaji	Elder sister
apna	"Own"; "own family"—father, mother, sister, brother, etc.; relatives
arain	Woman of vegetable grower caste
araiñ	Man of vegetable grower caste
Asuj	Sixth month of Punjabi calendar, middle of September to middle of October. (When spoken, pronounced *Asuñ*.)
azan	Muslim call to prayer
babu	A native clerk who writes and speaks English
bane da bhai	Brothers by having a common (land) boundary
barat	Wedding procession
barati	Members of wedding procession
barkat	Abundance; blessing
bebeji	Mother; see also *amaji*
Bhaduñ	Fifth month of Punjabi calendar, middle of August to middle of September. (When spoken, pronounced *Bhadreñ*.)
bhanji	Sweets
bid	Dried fruit and henna brought with *barat* to house of bride
biraderi	Patrilineage
Bisakh	First month of Punjabi calendar, middle of April to middle of May. (When spoken, pronounced *Vasakh*.)
bundi	Sweet pastry (a kind of sweetmeat).

* Spelled according to standard Oxford dictionary.

chapati	Native bread; a flat round cake made of unleavened dough
Chet	Twelfth month of Punjabi calendar, middle of March to middle of April. (When spoken, pronounced *Chetr.*)
chowdhrani	Wife or mother of *chowdhri*
chowdhri	Village chief, headman; honorary title for a *zamindar*
chowl	Money given by guests at *maiyañ* for *kammi* woman —barber's wife or mother; also at *khara* for barber and barber's wife or mother
chul	The hearth; money given at marriage by bridegroom's family to *kammis* of village of bride
dadke	Parental home (man speaking); parental home (married woman speaking, when visiting her *nanke*—her mother's mother's home); father's home and village (children speaking when visiting their *nanke*)
dayin	Village barber's wife or mother, who accompanies bride to parents-in-law for first time; midwife
ḍowli	Palanquin
dulin	Bride—one who comes in a palanquin
dupaṭa	Headcloth for women
gala	Ceremony officially opening wedding celebrations
ghar	House; household; household of *chowdhri*
ghar da jivai	Son-in-law of the house
ghar da kammi	*Kammis* of house
ghar di dhi	Daughter of the house
ghi	A liquid butter, clarified by boiling, made from the milk of cows and buffaloes
guṛ	Lumps of brown sugar
Haj	Pilgrimage to Mecca
*hakeem**	Native doctor
hakika	Ceremony on seventh, ninth, or eleventh day after birth of a child
Haṛ	Third month of Punjabi calendar, middle of June to middle of July
haṛi	Summer harvest, see *rabi*
hath phareda	*Jowra* (outfit of clothes) given to mother whose child is getting married; "plunging hands"
Hir Ranja	Romantic Punjabi poem
huka	Waterpipe
Id	Muslim religious holiday at the end of Ramzan
Id Milad	Festival of Nativity on twelfth day of the third lunar month of Muslim calendar

* Spelled according to standard Oxford dictionary.

Id-ul-Bakr	Muslim religious holiday one day after the Haj, when sheep is sacrificed
imam	Officiating priest of a mosque
izzet	Prestige, honor, status
jedi virsa	Land inherited from ancestors in the male line
Jeth	Second month of Punjabi calendar, middle of May to middle of June
jowra	Outfit of clothes for men and women
kabila	Altogether *biraderi*, patrilineage
kachi pini	Sweet pastry, loose mixture of rice flour, sugar, and *ghi*
kamiz	Tunic worn by a woman or a man
kammi	Craftsman
kasba	Larger village
Kashmiri	Descendants of immigrants from Kashmir; caste without special profession
Katak	Seventh month of Punjabi calendar, middle of October to middle of November. (When spoken, pronounced *Kateñ*.)
khara	Ritual bath taken by bride or bridegroom
khara lhai	Money, buffalo, or horse given to the groom or bride by *nanke* to get off washing plank at ritual bath
kharif	Autumn harvest, see also *sauni*
khichri	Rice cooked with lentils
kurum kurumni	Parents (4) of a married couple vis-à-vis
kuza	Small water vessel for ablutions, etc.
laag	Money received by *kammis* of house at ceremonies from the house they work for
laj	Honor; see also *pat* and *patlaj*
lamberdar	Revenue head of a village
lara	Bridegroom
lasi	Buttermilk
leda	Ceremony at death of old parent; also things brought at that ceremony
ledu	Pastry given at marriages, made of dough filled with almonds, raisins, coconut, sugar, and fried cream of wheat, fried in *ghi;* ceremony of distribution of *ledu* in village before marriage
lota	Metal vessel for ablutions, etc.
lungi	Wrap-around; specially woven cloth draped from waist to ankles, worn by men and women
Magh	Tenth month of Punjabi calendar, middle of January to middle of February. (When spoken, pronounced *Mañ*.)

Maghar	Eighth month of Punjabi calendar, middle of November to middle of December
maiyañ	Ceremony of tying bracelet of colored thread around wrist of bride or bridegroom
mamuñ	Mother's brother. (When spoken, pronounced *mamañ*.)
mang	Collective labor
mang·na	"To ask"
*maund****	Measure of weight; 1 *maund* equals 40 *seers* or approximately 82 pounds.
mekru	Unclean
mela	A country fair; festival held to commemorate anniversary of death of a holy person or a ruler
mera ghar	"My house," i.e., my family
meyl	Gathering of wedding guests
meyla	Mediation of a "daughter of the village" in a dispute
meyli	Wedding guests
mhendi	Henna; ceremony of putting henna on bride or bridegroom
mirasi	Village bard
mirasiñ	Wife of village bard
mithyai	Sweet pastry
Muharram	Month of mourning; first month of the Muslim calendar
muklawa	Second visit of bride or bridegroom to family of parents-in-law
muñh vekhan	Money given to a new-born child "to see the face"; also to bride (or bridegroom) by parents-in-law first time bridegroom (or bride) visits their house
musalli	Man of caste of agricultural laborer
musalliñ	Wife of musalli
nai	A barber
nanekwali	Gifts brought to bride by *nanke* for her dowry—*jowṛas*, bedding, copper, gold ornaments
nanke	Mother's parents' home and their village (man or woman speaking); mother's parents' home and their village (children speaking when in their *dadke*)
nanki virsa	Land inherited from mother's side
neondra	Money given to parents of bridegroom by male *meylis*
nikah	Ceremony of marriage contract
nuh	Daughter-in-law
obṛ	Non-kin, stranger; see also *opra*
opra	Non-kin, stranger; see also *obṛ*

* Spelled according to standard Oxford dictionary.

pagri	Man's turban
pak	Purified, blessed
panjiri	Loose mixture of cream of wheat and sugar fried in *ghi*
parea	Village council
pat	Honor; see also *laj* and *patlaj*
patlaj	Honor; see also *pat* and *laj*
patti	Section of a village, also section of village land, see *wand*
patwari	Government official, keeps land records and statistics of the village
peke	Married woman's paternal home
Phagan	Eleventh month of Punjabi calendar, middle of February to middle of March
phuphar	Father's sister's husband
phuphi	Father's sister
pilau	Salted rice cooked with meat and *ghi*
pir	Spiritual guide, a holy man
Poh	Ninth month of Punjabi calendar, middle of December to middle of January
prang	Daughters' daughters of mirasi's village married into another village
ptassa	Light sugar candy
rabi	Summer harvest; see also *hari*
Rabi-ul-Avval	Month of birth of Prophet Muhammad, third lunar month of Muslim calendar
Rajjab	Month of giving *zakat,* seventh month of Muslim calendar
Ramzan	Month of fasting, ninth month of Muslim calendar
ratha chari	"Knightly gesture" ceremony at marriage, when bridegroom's family in village of bride honors the daughters and daughters' daughters of other villages married into bridegroom's village
rishta	Connection through marriage
rishtadar	Total kin group, alternative *saak*
roti	Invitation to a meal at death of old person; the meal itself; also native bread, meal
*rupee**	Pakistani money. One *rupee* equals 16 *annas.* Value up to 1955: Rs. 3.3 = $1.00. Since 1955: Rs. 4.75 = $1.00.
saak	Total kin group; see *rishtadar*
sadr	Innermost desire

* Spelled according to standard Oxford dictionary.

Safar	Month of hardship, when charity should be done, second month of Muslim calendar
sagan	Coconut, almonds, and raisins or sweets given to a child on first visit to relatives as symbol of relationship; also to bride or bridegroom on first visit to spouse's relatives; also to bridegroom by *thehans*
Saif-ul-Mulk	Romantic Punjabi poem
sambhal	Cooked rice distributed to village at marriage
sauni	Autumn harvest; see also *kharif*
saure	Husband's home and village (wife speaking); wife's home and village (man speaking)
Sawan	Fourth month of Punjabi calendar, middle of July to middle of August. (When spoken, pronounced Saoñ.)
seer*	Measure of weight, 2 pounds
selami	Money given to welcome bride or bridegroom
serwarna	Money collected at a wedding for *kammi* women of house
seviyañ	Vermicelli
seyp	Work contract
seypi	Those who have contract
Shab-e-Barat	Religious celebration, two weeks before Ramzan
Shariat	Islamic law
shelwar	Baggy pants worn by men, women, children
sherif	Noble
Sohni Mehiñwal	Romantic Punjabi poem
sura	Section of the Koran
suratum mustakim	The straight path
tabaruk	Blessed food from the table of a *pir* or of a holy person
ṭabr	Family, also reference to patrilineage
tahmud	Draped cloth falling from waist to ankles, worn by men, women, children
tahsil	District subdivision
tahsildar	Assistant land revenue officer
tarwianda	Third visit of bride or bridegroom to family of parents-in-law
thehan	Gifts brought by bridegroom (with *barat*) to honor daughters of his village married in the village of the bride; also, the women so honored; means "same as daughter" and is derived from *dhi*, daughter
ṭika	Gold ornament worn on forehead. "Outstanding," e.g., *ṭika* village

* Spelled according to standard Oxford dictionary.

tonga	Horse and buggy
tongawala	Horse and buggy driver
urs	Anniversary of death of a *pir*
vaḍa	Big, great
vag pharai	"Holding the reins," money given by bridegroom to sisters and female cousins
var	Distribution of uncooked food in village before marriage (wheat and lentils or meat [mutton or beef])
varasui	Clothes and jewels brought to bride by bridegroom
vartan bhanji	System of reciprocal gift exchange
vartan	Dealing (*noun*)
vartna	To deal (*verb*)
vaṭo saṭa	Form of marriage in which a sister or a niece is given in exchange for a bride
vedaigi	Money given to a *kammi* who brings a wedding invitation and by hostess to *kammi* of guest
vehi	Family register for money given and received on ceremonial occasions
veyl	Gift of wheat brought to house of marriage by guests at *gala* and on *maiyañ*, given to *kammis* of the house who help (barber's wife and *musalliñ*)
	Also money given to musicians at wedding or circumcision by male guests
wanḍ	Section of a village, also section of village land; see also *patti*
zakat	Religious assessment of property
zamindar	Landowner
zat	Caste or identity

Bibliography

Calvert, H. *The Size and Distribution of Agricultural Holdings in the Punjab*. Lahore, 1925. The Board of Economic Inquiry, Punjab, Rural Section Publication No. 4.

Darling, M. L. *The Punjab Peasant in Prosperity and Debt*. London, Oxford University Press, 1925.

—— *Rusticus Loquitor or The Old Light and the New in the Punjab Village*. London, Oxford University Press, 1930.

—— *Wisdom and Waste in the Punjab Village*. London, Oxford University Press, 1934.

Dass, Anchal. *An Economic Survey of Gajju Chak, a Village in the Gujranwala District of the Punjab*. Lahore, 1934. The Board of Economic Inquiry, Punjab, Rural Village Surveys, No. 6.

Fyzee, Asaf A. A. *Outlines of Muhammadan Law*. London, Oxford University Press, 1949.

Gibb, H. A. R. *Mohammedanism: An Historical Survey*. New York, The New American Library, 1955.

Punjab. *Gazetteer of the Lahore District, 1883–84*. Calcutta, 1884.

—— *Punjab District Gazetteers*, Vol. XXV–A. Lahore, 1921.

Ibbetson, D. C. J. *Report on the Census of the Punjab Taken on the 17th February, 1881*. Vol. I. Calcutta, 1883.

Maron, S., Ed. *Pakistan: Society and Culture*. New Haven, Human Relations Area Files, 1957. Behavior Science Monographs.

Marriott, McK., Ed. *Village India: Studies in the Little Community*. American Anthropological Association, 1955. Comparative Studies of Cultures and Civilizations, No. 6, Memoir No. 83.

Qureshi, I. H. *The Pakistani Way of Life*. London, Heinemann, 1956.

Redfield, R. *The Little Community: Viewpoints for the Study of a Human Whole*. Chicago, University of Chicago Press, 1955.

—— *Peasant Society and Culture: An Anthropological Approach to Civilization*. Chicago, University of Chicago Press, 1956.

Report of the Basic Principles Committee (as adopted by the Constituent Assembly on 21 September 1954); *Interim Report of the Committee on the Fundamental Rights of Citizens of Pakistan and on Matters Relating to Minorities* (as adopted by the Constituent Assembly of Pakistan on 6 October 1950); *Report of the Committee on the Fundamental Rights of Citizens of Pakistan and on Matters Relating to Minorities* (as adopted by the Constituent Assembly of Pakistan on 7 September 1954). Karachi, Government of Pakistan Press, 1954.

Smith, M. W., "The *Misal:* A Structural Village-Group of India and Pakistan," *American Anthropologist,* Vol. LIV, No. 1 (January-March, 1952).

Thorner, D., and A. Thorner, "India and Pakistan," in *Most of the World,* Ralph Linton, Ed. New York, Columbia University Press, 1949.

Wallbank, T. W. *A Short History of India and Pakistan, from Ancient Times to the Present.* New York, The New American Library, 1958.

Index

Straight path (*suratum mustakim*), 71
String, knotted, 87
Sugarcane, 55
Summer, harvest and planting, 52, 204
Sweetmaker, professional, 146
Sweets, in *vartan bhanji*, 97; distribution of, 107, 197; weighed and counted, 125, 132; presented at marriage ceremonies, 143–48; money as substitute for, 161

Tabaruk, 72
Tahmud, 63
Tahsildar, see under Revenue official
Tailor, modern occupations of, 184 f.
Talwandi, village, 159; land relinquished by women, 188 f.
Taxes, in cash, 2; household, 26
Tenant farmer, 31, 44; rise in status, 194
Textile plants, 179
Theft, attitude of *biraderi* toward guilty man, 79 f.
Thehan, 83, 111 f., 141, 169, 210 f., 217
Tika, 114
Timber, market, 12; machine sawn, 181
Tree, planting of, 43

Urdu language, xiii f.
Urs, 70
Usufructuary rights, in houses, 43

Vag pharai, see under Money
Valuables, hidden, 24; given on special occasions, 171 f.
Var, ceremony, 149, 212
Vartan bhanji, exchange of gifts and services, xi; household distinctions re, 26; training for participation in, 88; strengthening of family ties, 89, 94 f.; in marriage ceremonies, 91 ff.; on visits to parents-in-law, 97; equilibrium in, 101; meaning of term, 105; meaning of practice, 105–7; bases of, 106 f.; rules, 106, 109, 122–33, 138 ff.; scale of, 107,

128, 136, 149, 158; initiation of, 112, 160; rule of reciprocity (*q.v.*), 114 f.; dual transaction, 115 n; 125 ff.; groups involved, 116–21; degrees of relationship, 117, 156; amount and quality of gifts, 119; types of gifts (*q.v.*), 120 f., 143 f.; social and economic aspects, 127 ff.; examples of relationships, 130–32; series of transactions, 136 f., 174 f.; breach of rules, 139; factors governing scale of, 173; category of recipients, 175; groups concerned with, 176; changes in, 194 ff.
Vato sata, 83 f., 91, 187
Vedaigi, 163
Vegetable growers (*arains*), 18, 61
Vehi, see Family register
Vendors, itinerant, 63
Veyl, 140, 141, 149
Village council (*parea*), 17, 30; settlement of disputes, 31; intervillage work of, 198
Villages, social and economic changes in, 3; new, settlement of, 3; emigration from, and return to, 4, 178; character of, 7; daily life, 8; size of, 13, 17; intervillage ties, 16, 138; craftsmen shared by, 17; types of, 21; social life, 30 f., 56, 62, 65; section of (*patti; wand*), 43, 46; struggle for power, 46 f.; itinerant visitors, 63; permanence of ties with, 77 f., 178 ff.; linked through intervillage marriages, 111; *tika*, 114; distribution of food in, 149, 197; adaptation to innovations, 185 f.; boy's marriage with city girl, 193; participation in marriage ceremonies, 196, 210, 212–14; interrelationships, 198 f.

Wazirabad, town, 11 f., 20
Weaver, 35, 54, 57; as headmaster, 17; changes in craft of, 179
Wedding guests (*meyli*), 117; gifts to, 125, 141, 154 ff., 162, 168, 197; invitations to, 145; at bridegroom's house, 146 f.; in bride's house, 147, 155, 219; food for, 150 f.; gathering